KEYS TO NATIONAL RECOVERY

PREPARING THE NATION FOR GREATNESS

ZACK ROBERTS

authorHOUSE®

AuthorHouse™
1663 Liberty Drive
Bloomington, IN 47403
www.authorhouse.com
Phone: 1 (800) 839-8640

Published by AuthorHouse 09/15/2017

ISBN: 978-1-5462-0635-4 (sc)
ISBN: 978-1-5462-0634-7 (e)

Library of Congress Control Number: 2017913290

Print information available on the last page.

This book is printed on acid-free paper.

To the leaders of the previous generation of this great nation Liberia, whose legacy has one way or the other provided lessons that inspire and warn.

Praise be to Yahweh for the lesson we have learned from you on what to do and what not to do. To the leaders of the present generation who will keep their hearts and minds open to champion the moved of Yahweh to fulfill the divine purposes for this great nation and who dare to make a difference and realize that the dignity and quality of the future of Liberia rest upon you.

To my friends, mentors, and Pastor John Gallinger, who inspired me to believe that it is possible to be effective in having an impact on education and to contribute meaningfully with my talent, gifts, and personal life.

To the leaders and co-laborers of Strong Tower Assembly, who always make me feel that there is a call of Yahweh upon my life and who have built their trust and confidence in me as their pastor. Yahweh bless you all.

CONTENTS

FOREWORD

Insight

Africa is rich and loaded with diverse natural minerals, some of which cannot be found on any other continent. Her people have been locked in abject poverty decade after decade, and the land of our nation has become a bloody battlefield. At the same time, there are nations that have fewer or no mineral resources, and yet their people enjoy a higher standard of living and breathe the air of peace.

Why? Why? Why?

No nation of the world ever became great by chance. If you browse the history of every great nation, you will discover organized principles that were carefully calculated and carved out by their founders and systematically implemented and followed by their citizens.

Africa by contrast has been a land of selfishness, greed, and personal agendas. Time and time again, men who ascend to power in our land pursue their own goals and then leave their people lingering in the belly of extreme poverty, diseases, and illiteracy. This book is an eye-opener filled with both natural and divine wisdom to emancipate this nation and any nation crying out for national redirection. We salute the author, Pastor Zack Roberts.

—Bishop Jonathan F. Foxx Sr.
Senior Prelate at Revival Center International
Republic of Liberia

PREFACE

Dear reader,

This book is for ambitious people who want to recover from past failures and losses and to get ahead faster. If this is your intention, then I believe you are the person for whom this book was written. I will use the analogy of the coin in this life-changing book. The coin has two sides depicting the dual nature of life, internal and external, and it is an obvious symbol of prosperity and wealth. On one side of the coin are people who have caused immeasurable destruction within this nation. They lack vision. They are corrupt, dishonest people who still have the mind to ruin this great nation. And on the other side of the coin lies Liberia's future, success, failure, life, and death, waiting for someone like Nehemiah to seek its welfare. The side of the coin that you are on determines how far this nation will go.

The ideas contained in the pages ahead outlined keys to national recovery that will save the nation years of unnecessary struggle and hardship in achieving the goals that are most important. By following the steps explained in the pages ahead, the nation will move to the front of the line. Friends, this book is meant to be a road map or a life guide to help the nation gets where it should be. As it is often said, paraphrased, "A journey of a thousand miles begins with a single step." The curtain is drawn, closing on the old and opening to the new Liberia in a new season. This is our opportunity for a fresh start, a bold approach, and a new vision.

Friends, there will be a lot of changes and shifts in the spiritual realm, and these will affect the physical realm and all the spheres of life in this new Liberia. The old system will cease its operation. Many people will be shocked, especially those who thought they could keep this country in failure. While you are reading, I'd like you to consider the law of cause and effect. It says that there is always a cause for every effect. In life, success is not an accident; failure is not an accident either.

As you read this book, Yahweh Almighty will give you more wisdom, knowledge, and understanding on your journey. In Yahshua's mighty name, amen.

ACKNOWLEDGMENTS

We are the sum total of all the individuals who have in one way or another, small or great, influenced and contributed to our lives. A book is never the result of one person.

I have studied the lives of others and learned everything I know from someone. We are all products of what we have acquired and gained from other people.

I thank the many friends, educators, authors, and family members whose lives have influenced and contributed to mine. Thanks to Patrick Johnson, CEO of Star-Vision, for his enthusiastic response to my ideas. He helped me focus my efforts in writing this book and in the editing process.

This work is a contribution and product of these many minds. I am especially grateful to Juliet Amaefule in Nigeria, who helped me type the first manuscript.

A special thanks to my wife, Faith Cecilia Roberts, for her patience and understanding. My attention temporarily shifted away from her while I was writing this book. Her support provided the encouragement I needed to finish this book.

INTRODUCTION

This is a wonderful time to be alive. There have never been more opportunities for creative and determined Liberians to achieve the desire of personal and national recovery today, regardless of the short-term ups and downs in the country and in your personal life. I believe by faith, we have entered a time of sober reflection to review and gather the past of our years of failure as a currency to invest it into the future that is in its preparatory stage. We cannot afford to sacrifice and squander the future of our beloved nation any longer. I do believe this time, from a biblical perspective, is right for stirring up our national recovery that is superior to any previous era in our nation's history. National recovery is a dream so we must wakeup to make it a reality so that we don't lost our nation. Joseph had a dream that caused Egypt to understand economics while the rest of the world was in collapsed without an economic plan. You will agree economics plays a key role in the prosperity and peace of every nation (Gen 37:5-9). We cannot recovery nationally just by hoping that things will get better. Things will get better when we as a nation strategically and meticulously plan with better decision and right actions for the restoration of broken lives. It will not be a smooth series of progressive steps. There will be many ups and downs marked by occasional successes and temporary failures. Thus, by reading this book, you will acquire keys to national recovery.

During this process of national recovery, you must not be afraid to learn and use the lessons from your past failures. The past can inspire collective actions that can help us build a progressive future. I believed we are the generation that will set the standards and become an indispensable voice in the nation. One reason people, institutions, businesses, and governments fail is because those in authority do not meet the standard that they demand from others. Our leaders are the architects of the fortune of this nation, and they are also the architects of the misfortune of this nation. Nobody is a stumbling block to us. We are our own stumbling blocks.

Our leaders need to be proactive in thinking ahead of the people they lead. If they are not proactive, the people will be reactive. That is why we have all kinds of negative behaviors. The first law of Sir Isaac Newton states that anything that is not moving will be static unless a force is applied. As Liberians, we need to take action now and move with the times because if we do not move with the times or catch up with the world, the world will move without us.

Hopefully, this book will showcase our belief that national recovery is not possible without righteousness. Proverbs 14:34 says, "Righteousness exalts a nation but sin is reproach to any people" Proverbs 8:20–21 says, "I lead in the way of righteousness. In the midst of the paths of judgment; that I may cause those that love me to inherit substance, and I will fill their treasures." Liberia's history as a nation has clearly spelled this out for all us who have intrinsically understood the rot in Liberia and how the nation has failed woefully in the past despite the potential riches within her grasp.

Obviously, there is a need to teach people how to succeed in life, given the ravages of the failure out there. There is an even greater need for us to learn how we can help to create the change leading to national recovery within our nation. There is ardent yearning for that change in our nation today. I hope this book will enable all Liberians who are intensely enthusiastic about recovery. I prophesy that Liberia will be blessed with great leaders who will lead this nation to national recovery, prosperity, and success, beginning with the national leaders. "Men, women boys and girls with a vision to achieve their purpose(s) must realize that it's always a welcome truth that righteousness pays great dividend in national recovery" (Zack Roberts).

CHAPTER 1

Getting Started

We need a paradigm shift to get started. In 1962, Thomas Kuhn wrote that a paradigm shift is a change from one way of thinking to another. It is a revolution, a transformation, a sort of metamorphosis. It does not just happen, but driven by agents of change. In this context, those of us who want change must become the agents of change. The sensible thing to do before we get started is to learn more about our country so that we can begin our work toward the new Liberia.

Why have we become a people of corrupt minds, destitute, and impoverished, swayed as a country? Why have we been so poorly defined if we are going to recover? I firmly believe the reason we fall into chaos is that of bad leadership. That is what happened to the children of Israel in Judges 17:6. In those days there was no king (leader) in Israel. In Liberia, every man did what was right in his own eyes. Judges 21:25This sad and pathetic story repeated is in.

Cursed is the nation without a true leader. This situation can be likened to a body without a head. I think God is showing us where we have fallen.

> For, behold, the Lord, the Lord of host, doth take away from Jerusalem and from Judah the stay and staff, the whole stay of bread, and the whole stay of water. The mighty man, and the man of war, the Judge, and the prophet, and the prudent, and the ancient, the captain of the fifty, and the honorable man, and the counselor,

> and the cunning artificer, and the eloquent orator. And I will give children to be their princes, and babes shall rule over them. And the people shall be oppressed, everyone by another, and everyone by his neighbor; the child shall behave himself proudly against the ancient, and the base against the honorable. When a man shall take hold of his brother of the house of his father, saying, Thou hast clothing, be thou our ruler, and let this ruin be under thy hand: in that day shall he swear, saying, I will not be a healer; for in my house is neither bread nor clothing: make me not a ruler of the people. As for my people, children are their oppressors, and women rule over them. O my people, they which lead thee cause thee to err, and to destroy the way of thy paths. (Isaiah 3:1–7, 12)

The lack of true leadership gives rise to the proliferation of greed, corruption, and oppression as we have seen in the scriptures. Like Israel, it is a pattern we have followed. Almost every ugly situation within the nation can be attributed to people with childish and irresponsible attitudes. Friends, God is real; He gives us an account in the scripture we just read. God said He would bring a curse upon the land by removing leaders. As another translation puts it in verse 5: "And the people will be oppressed, each one by another and each one by his neighbor, and the youth will storm against the elder and the inferior against the honorable." This scripture shows a clear picture of a society where oppression, injustice, crimes, lawlessness, intimidation, and the proliferation of all sorts of wickedness reigns. Similarly, our leaders are not children in terms of age, but children in their mentalities, in their behaviors, and in their actions. This picture of child-like leadership represents incapable and foolish leaders. The impacts and effects of child-like leadership are reaffirmed in Ecclesiastes 10:16–17 "Woe to you, O land, whose king (leader) is a lad and whose princes feast in the morning. Blessed are you, O land, whose king (leader) is of nobility and whose princes eat at the appropriate time—for strength and not for drunkenness."

There is a need for a new genuine leadership that will unite the nation; because one of the key requirements for us is to find like-minded people for the common good of the country, is to see everyone as Liberians and not by tribes. A new leadership that will lead the citizens under the Constitution, leadership that will protect our unique brand called Liberia, leadership that will stand up for our sovereignty, and leadership that will encourage a progressive society. Like the nation, Isreal pointed out in Nehemiah 2:17; 4:6 "Then I said to them, You see the bad situation we are in: Jerusalem [Liberia] is desolate and its gates burned by fire. Come let us rebuild the wall of Jerusalem [Liberia] so that we will no longer be a reproach." "So, we built the wall, and the whole wall was joined together to half its height for the people had a mind to work." This new leadership should understand that the success or failure of our national recovery efforts will be determined primarily based on its genuineness to lead.

Moreover, there is a high need for constitutional reform that will guide the new leadership because the values and the principles that point the nation to national recovery, from the very beginning, must be enshrined in the reformed constitution. The success of making Liberia great should be rooted and defined in our proposed reformed Constitution. As a nation coming out of obscurity, we need leadership that will awaken our national consciousness. At this point in our nation's history, it is recommended that we study existing and well-established countries who have gone through major reforms to determine all that made them successful that we can learn from them. As an elected official, you potentially have the power to make a difference in your country. It is not just the ability to speak persuasively and effectively in front of a crowd but also capacity to gain the confidence and assurance of the people you lead. This includes how you fulfill the expectations of your elected.

Specifically, If we intend to function as an independent country, we will ultimately need to improve our infrastructures (e.g., building good roads and schools, hospitals, and fire stations). Politics can be a challenging and rewarding profession. role and showcase your passion for change.

Getting started will need research and insight into the decisions of earlier leadership to identify some of the worst-case scenarios that brought catastrophe to us; this will help us to understand the source of the problem. The purpose of this book is to help remedy the effects of current and past government actions through ongoing scrutiny to avoid the pitfalls that have contributed to the nation's downfall and to shape the future of the new Liberia.

Preparing the country for greatness also aims to unify the citizens within the nation so that they remain politically and economically stable and benefit future generations. We must embark upon national campaigns to repair the shattered infrastructures and broken lives. Keys to national recovery refer to government policies designed to foster the keen sense of national identity lost for years. All of this is geared toward changing our country's outlook and creating national trust. We must set up and secure national goals.

Concerning nations, David confesses, "Blessed is the nation whose God is the Lord, the people whom he has chosen as his heritage." (Psalm 33:12). The destiny of our country depends on our obedience to the Word of God. To prepare for greatness, we must be prepared to obey the precepts that the Bible instructs us to do just as David did. The biblical worldview is the only basis for political freedom. The historical fact is that our freedom as a people comes directly out of the biblical view of politics and from no other source. The law and the grace of God are the only substantial support for that freedom we want to enjoy.

I firmly believe we have what it takes to become a great nation—a nation that can make things happen for our people. This book is written to help us recognize the enormous potential that we have as a peculiar group of people and to develop and refine the characteristics needed to be a great nation. Every nation depends on its leadership. But every nation rises and falls based on its leaders. God commands people to submit to the existing authorities. He also provides safeguards against misrule and has several commands for those in power to follow. "Now listen to this Warning, you Kings; [leaders] learn this lesson, you rulers of the world: Serve the Lord with fear, tremble and bow down to him: or Else his anger will be quickly aroused, and you will suddenly die." (Psalm 2:10–12).

God has given us everything, so there is no reason why we should be so economically and politically unproductive. There exist in this nation largely untapped and unexplored resources that can make a growing impact.

This is the platform on which to begin our journey to national recovery. Liberians are looking for leaders who will make an indelible impact. God said to David in 1 Chronicles 17:7 just as he is saying to our leaders today. "Now, therefore, thus shall you say to My servant David, put your name there, 'Thus says the LORD of hosts, "I took you from the pasture, from following the sheep, to be leader over My people Israel [Liberia]." Liberia's destiny hangs on its leadership. It is time for us to reflect, review, and renew our commitment. Let's examine leaders who intend to impact history because it takes a great leader to lead a great nation.

I want to encourage you to keep reading this book over and over, keep addressing the issues we're dealing with in the pages of this book. We have looked at the past, we see the present, and we now want to move into the future. Remember the words of John Maxwell "everything rises and falls on leadership." Bernard Montgomery, the British field marshal, said, "Leadership is the capacity and will to rally men and women to a common purpose and the character which inspires confidence." On this note, an old parable paraphrased about a fish - "Give me a true leader with a heart for Liberia, and I will populate the nation with great people with like minds for generations to come."

CHAPTER 2

A Look at Our Economy

The economy of Liberia encompasses all activities related to production, consumption, trade of goods, and services. The economy in this context applies to everyone from individuals to entities such as corporations and the government. As a nation, our economy is to be governed by our culture, laws, history, and geography among other factors, and it evolves because of how it is properly managed. The study of economics and the factors affecting the economy is called economics. The discipline of economics can be broken into two primary areas of focus— (1) microeconomics and (2) macroeconomics. Microeconomics studies the behavior of individuals and firms to understand why they make the economic decisions they do and how these decisions affect the larger economic system. Macroeconomics, on the other hand, studies the entire economy, focusing on large-scale decisions and issues, including unemployment and gross domestic product (GDP).

Many politicians are obsessed with money yet understand little of the workings of economics. The first and most fundamental economic principle that we need to grasp is simply this; God owns everything. He says if we keep his commandment, things will go well for us in the land. Isaiah 1:19 says, "If ye be willing and obedient, ye shall eat the good of the land:" Sproul provides historical evidence that "nations most influenced by biblical Christianity are nations that, by and large, have prospered. They are nations marked by decentralized governments and free markets. But nations that reject God are marked by centralized power, tyranny, and no free markets." "the land of Canaan; as the Jews held the possession of that land, before the times of Christ, by their obedience to the laws of God, which were given them as a body politic, and which, so long as they observed, they were continued in the quiet and full enjoyment of all the blessings of it; so, when Christ came, had they received, embraced, and acknowledged him as the Messiah, and been obedient to his will, though only externally, they would have remained in their own land, and enjoyed all the good things in it undisturbed by enemies."

We know God's moral principles, the Ten Commandments, as revealed in Exodus 20 and Deuteronomy 5, but how can economic principles be discovered? Surely, the scientific method of trial and error does not exclude what is revealed by biblical knowledge. To even suggest that moral principles could be relevant in the study of economic phenomena would be rejected as a serious breach of scientific method and purity. Moreover, continuous experimentation and the formation of hypotheses like we are doing today cannot produce anything but "tentative principles."

"The Greek word for basic principles means "primary and fundamental principles of any art, science, or discipline." While the apostle Paul was specifically warning the Colossians against agnosticism, his admonition applies to all areas of scientific endeavor, including the discipline of economics. We must build on the ultimate foundation, God's Word, the Bible, not on any worldly paradigm. Our basic principles must come from the Bible." We know from experience that our nation's economy is fractured into many competing traditions, causing the economic collapse accompanied by social chaos, civil unrest, and sometimes a breakdown of law and order. If we want to make sense of our economy, then we need to go back many years into our past to find out what the word economy means.

Don G. Boland from the Centre for Thomistic Studies says, "Economics is a word made up from two Greek words okionomia and nomos." The first refers to a household. Though in ancient times, this referred to something more extensive than the modern household. It could signify a large estate or even a village. The second word means distribution or management, and it was derived from nemein, meaning "to distribute, manage." There are two ideas here. There is a general one of ordering. "As such, any ordered system came to be referred to as an economy (e.g., the celestial economy). The other more particular idea is one related to (the ordering of) human affairs (i.e., a conscious adaptation of means to end) so that we adhere to the avoidance of waste. More particularly still, we focus on the day-to-day affairs of people and their livelihoods." (Boland, 1997)

A study conducted by John Robinson says that "the purpose of studying economics is not to acquire a set of ready-made answers to economic questions but to learn how to avoid being deceived by economists." Economy refers to the management of the home or household management. Words like economy or ecology help us understand the responsibility that our government has in the economics of our nation. How can we move toward a more sustainable and efficient solution?

This topic is designed to make us think critically and analytically to warn us about the fast-approaching destruction of our economy. It is like a map, and those who are wise enough to read the signs written in this book can escape. We must make some changes to avert collapse. Now just because the economy has not crashed yet does not mean it cannot, but if we can make some adjustments for expansion, our economic conditions will change. I trust that my insights are from the Lord. He can give direction and help our government prepare now. Consider an earthquake. Earthquakes do not just happen; they happened through specific geological forces working that result in eruptions on the surface. Hence, this does not require a geological wizard to see there is an economic eruption going on in Liberia.

You will be surprised to find out how much the Bible says about economic issues. In Liberia, we should not feel that the word economics is outside the domain of our nation. If anything, we need to recapture this problem and bring out a strong biblical answer. I believe this knowledge will empower people to do wonderful things in Liberia. I also believe that we should not have to put our lives on hold to gain this knowledge. Our government's mission should be to make sure that our people have access to quality information about the economy even when they suffer from challenging life circumstances. Our leaders should be there to help us achieve our personal and professional economic goals. Because of the massive decline in law and order and its devastating effects we have suffered, nobody seems to know where the Liberian economy is heading. So, it is time to return to the basics when it comes to our economy.

Transformation and national recovery will only happen when we return to scripture to see what God has to say about economics. Let us consider the sharp decline in the areas of honesty and accountability because of selfish and greed, Liberia's economy is amid an epic collapse. There is an increasing need for our leaders to constrain self-interest and make things work for the common good of the nation. I believe if we wisely and biblically control self-interest, it will generate significant economic prosperity and freedom for the citizens Consider Luke 3:10–11.

> And the crowds were questioning him saying, "Then what shall we do?" And he would answer and say to them, "The man who has two tunics is to share with him who has none; and he who has food is to do likewise. And some tax collectors also came to be baptized, and they said to him, "Teacher, what shall we do?" And he said to them, "Collect no more than what you have been ordered to." some soldiers were questioning him, saying, "And what about us, what shall we do?" And he said to them, "Do not take money from anyone by force, or accuse anyone falsely, and be content with your wages."

We are looking for sound biblical solutions for economic issues so that our nation can function correctly. Popularly said "the ends justify the means," but I respectfully disagree because that statement is not biblical and ungodly. I would say the means justify the ends. When people get to power, they use their positions or offices to feed their greed.

> And constant friction between men of depraved mind and deprived of the truth, who suppose that godliness is a means of gain. But godliness is a means of great gain when accompanied by contentment, for we have brought nothing into the world, so we cannot take anything out of it either." If we have food and covering with these, we shall be content. "But those who want to get rich fall into temptation and a snare and many foolish and harmful desires which plunge men into ruin and destruction. for the love of money is a root of all sorts of evil, and some by longing for it have wandered away from the faith and

> pierced themselves with many griefs. (1 Timothy 6:5–10, New American Standard Bible).

The historical echo of our past and present offers an opportunity for those of us who are eager to understand where the future of the Liberian economy goes from here. We need to ask ourselves what will make an impact on the Liberian economy because the lives of our citizens are being abandoned. We have fallen prey to thieves and psychopaths in leadership, which has brought about severe distress on the citizens; this is part of the sinfulness that keeps us revising history, which only dilutes the lessons we should learn from it. The solution is not just to change the economic system but to change the human nature that is corrupting the economic system. We must use the gospel. But I can hear God saying by faith in John 10:10, "The thief comes only to steal and kill and destroy; I came that they may have life, and have it abundantly." God says the silver is mine, and the gold is mine, declares the LORD."

Since the 1990s, the Liberian economy has had a negative impact on its citizens. The result is eroding public trust. Many believed the illusion that running a nation's economy is like child's play. Whenever you hear the word economy, remember that it simply means the management of a home. In this case, it refers to a nation as the home. Now we want to go a little deeper in understanding the origin of the word economics. The word economics is derived from a Greek word okionomia, which means "household management" or "management of house affairs" (i.e., how people earn income and resources and how they spend them on their necessities, comforts, and luxuries). With the passage of time, the word okionomia was used for an economy (i.e., how a nation takes steps to fulfill its desires and preferences with the help of limited means). That's why economics was called political economy in the early age.

Taking a deeper look at the ways things are, it is true that the weak Liberian dollar has not ignited an export boom for us, and it will not even in the foreseeable future. It is disheartening to see Liberians go through this traumatic economic meltdown. At times, I am pessimistic about the future of the Liberian dollar and the economy because of a lack of confidence in our leaders. Liberia is not poor; she has a complex leadership problem.

With all of these situations, there can be a shift in the economy of the new Liberia that can make a significant impact. The government runs in a circle and gets stuck in a broken economy and thinks that our problems will resolve themselves. Politicians forget that their positions require honesty and accountability to manage an economy efficiently. The change in government should inspire confidence and renew our expectation to bring economic prosperity to the ordinary Liberians, who have suffered so much at the hands of those in power. Officials continue to mismanage the resources because of their bloodthirsty rule; they have succumbed to greed, lust for young girls and boys, and booze.

We need leaders who will put the people before profits. There is a need to remove the old system that prioritizes the exploitation of people's labor with a system that recognizes all wealth comes through work and rewards people accordingly. 2 Thessalonians 3:10 says, "For even when we were with you, we used to give you this order; if anyone is not willing to work, then he is not to eat either." I firmly believe that government must create jobs and encourage people to take their works or jobs seriously and apply this principle toward economic well-being. The government needs to rethink and restructure the way people think about ownership because people and communities own resources.

Our country is a representative democratic republic, and it was established on Christian principles. The government's values should reflect the values of the majority of its people. The government's values should also reflect the government officials themselves.

The role of the government is to enhance growth and stability of the economy. It gives the infrastructure and system that facilitate economic activity while formulating regulations and controls to ensure order and fairness in business operations. Our government exists to devise rules that ensure businesses operate with the best interests of the public in mind.

CHAPTER 3

History Repeats Itself

The proverb "History repeats itself" was stated all the way back to around the 1500s BC, although the English phrase itself is only five hundred years old according to my research. When we look at today, we see children often making the same mistakes their parents made in the past. One good thing about God is that he makes all things beautiful in his time. Paul had an understanding from God's perspective that we could often make the same mistakes of the past generations, so God made known to us that we can and should learn from history's mistakes. Apostle Paul had this in mind when he wrote, "Now all these things happened to them as examples, and they were written for our admonition, upon whom the ends of the ages have come. Therefore, let him who thinks he stands take heed lest he fall" (1 Corinthians 10:11–12). But at the same time, God wants us to be wise and observe what happened in the past and learn from those instances. That's why God gives us the Bible—to learn and avoid those mistakes. God's people in the Old Testament struggled with most of the things we are struggling with today—morality, pride, materialism, selfishness, etc. While we consider some of the mistakes we struggle with, let me share this scripture with you. "Woe to those who add house to house and join field to field until there is no more room, so that you have to live alone" (Isaiah 5:8).

In all this, God has given us tools that we can utilize to overcome the temptation of repeating - the same mistakes our predecessors made. The church cannot continue to repeat the mistake of taking handouts from the government because it will not be able to speak against corruption in government. Likewise, the government cannot continue to repeat all that brought us and keep us where we are as a nation. The church has given the government the freedom to mismanage our affairs. God tells us in his Word that history does not always have to repeat itself. "No temptation has overtaken you except such as is common to man. But God is faithful; who will not allow you to be tempted beyond what you are able, but with the temptation will also make the way of escape, that you may be able to bear" (1 Corinthians10:13).

When you learn from your mistakes, they become a source of strength that will help you see the value of your past. We can never change the past; work our present to fix the future through the mishaps of life. They can make you stronger and better. The children of today need to know about the history of this country, and this involves the parents and grandparents getting involved.

According to Wikipedia, the online encyclopedia, the word history comes ultimately from the ancient Greek term historia, meaning "inquiry, knowledge from inquiry, or judge." Genuine history is based on the investigation of facts to decide realities. Pastor Wayne Banks of Pleasant Green Missionary Baptist Church says, "History is not mere narrow-minded or close-minded propaganda that most governments funnel into children's minds so that they can parrot the same government-serving 'patriotic' fiction as their parents, or governments controlling a population through 'social engineering.' (i.e., brainwashing) people to think that they are originated from someone or something that they did not; thereby, turning people into easily manipulated "ego addicts." The second meaning of the word parrot refers to a person who mindlessly repeats the words or imitates the actions of another.

There is a quote from George Santayana that says, "Those who cannot remember the past are condemned to repeat it." According to that statement, repeating past mistakes brings condemnation upon us and contributes to the vicious cycle of breaking down our life and society. Let us look at the children of Israel in the book of Judges. Judges 2:16–23 says,

> Then the Lord raised up judges who delivered them from the hands of those who plundered them. Yet they did not listen to their judges, for they played the harlot after

> other gods and bowed themselves down to them. They turned aside quickly from the way in which their fathers had walked in obeying the commandments of the Lord; they did not do as their fathers. When the Lord raised up judges for them, the Lord was with the judge and delivered them from the hand of their enemies all the days of the judge; for the Lord was moved to pity by their groaning because of those who oppressed and afflicted them. But it came about when the judge died, that they would turn back and act more corruptly than their fathers, in following other gods to serve them and bow down to them; they did not abandon their practices or their stubborn ways. "So, the anger of the Lord burned against Israel, and He said, because this nation has transgressed my covenant which I commanded their fathers and has not listened to my voice, I also will no longer drive out before them any of the nations which Joshua left when he died, in order to test Israel by them, whether they will keep the way of the Lord to walk in it as their fathers did, or not. So the Lord allowed those nations to remain, not driving them out quickly; and He did not give them into the hand of Joshua.

Proverbs 26:11 says "Like a dog that returns to its vomit, is a fool who repeats his folly." Though we know it to be folly and ruinous to us, vice has become second nature, and we cannot escape from it. The dog is a loathsome emblem of those sinners who return to their vices as a dog returns to his vomit after he is sick. He casts it out again and then returns to lick it up. Those who repeat the mistakes of the past are described as dogs and fools; this is the situation in Liberia today. Can you picture yourself in this description? Let us look at the word folly, meaning "lack of good sense, understanding, or foresight, and stupidity." Another word we can look at is "vice," meaning "immoral or wicked behavior, corruption, misconduct, and misdeeds."

Let us get an understanding of what history is before we move on. History is the study of past events, particularly in human affairs. History repeats itself when we do not learn from our mistakes. We know this by observing our current situation and by tracing our problems back in our past. For example, a government comes to power and repeats the mistakes of the previous administration which is a clear manifestation of history repeating itself. We have seen on many occasions where citizens voted representatives into offices with the intent to represent their interest; instead, these officials misrepresent the people's interest. This situation has become a pattern. If we did a careful analysis to see the trend, we would see the steps that led us to repeat these mistakes. Undeniably, history repeats itself even in our own lives, and it causes the same problems in the lives of our children's children. When this happens, something unexpected always occurs.

One of the primary elements that has become a repetition or pattern in our nation is corruption. Corruption has damaged our society and has changed the fabrics of the nation. Albert Einstein said, "We can't solve problems by using the same kind of thinking we used when we created them." We must look and see if the same sets of events that have led to the breakdown of our society are still prevalence. We must keep surveillance on the issue of corruption to prevent it from happening because any society that breeds and nurtures corruption is set for no development and growth. Unless we find innovative ways of doing things, our lives are still in a repeat of the past. We observed, when people rise to power, they do not learn from history's mistakes; as a result, they get corrupted by power and forget the very essence for which they were given power. Therefore, the struggle with corruption has become a pattern regime after regime.

Another history of "repeat" in Liberia is the issues of failure. Edmond Burke advised, "Those who cannot remember the past are condemned to repeat it." This philosophy does not ensure that we will not make mistakes, but there are no problems with trying a better way after failures. Failure is not the end of Liberia, a glorious land of liberty. Many great names in the Bible had their failures, "And we know that in all things God works for the good of those who love him, who have been called according to his purpose" (Romans 8:28, New International Version). It is never too late to start over after failing yet starting right is important. As one author rightly said, insanity: doing the same thing repeatedly and expecting different results. We cannot keep doing the wrong thing and hope to get a different or better result; we must learn from the past to avoid similar mistakes.

I encourage you to get out of the comfort zone and stop repeating your past mistakes. The comfort zone is defined as "a psychological state in which a person feels familiar." The greatest benefit of learning from our past mistakes is realizing our future without letting the past influence it. Like we mentioned early, the past is something that we can never change nor should we try to change it. However, without it, we would not have learned the lessons we needed to learn. President Theodore Roosevelt said, "The only man who never makes a mistake is the man who never does anything." The mistakes we are experiencing as a nation should immediately indicate to us that something has gone wrong. This book is written to help prepare us to deal with the situations our country faced. Notwithstanding, most importantly, we must be ready to learn from the mistakes to improve our choices, decisions, and actions in the future.

Financial independence is critical to our national well-being. Being financially independent means that the more money the government handles, the more accountable she is expected else the government will tumble. History should not repeat itself in our country on the subject of financial independence. Over the years our leadership has not been able adequately to manage the financial system of our nation. We have become champions only to memorize historical dates, and names, and events, and not the lessons they teach. I believe that in an educated society with a well-run government, history should not repeat itself when it comes to the issue of financial mismanagement. But this is only possible by demonstrating a higher level of responsibility, accountability, and transparency. Our leaders need to guard their integrity as a sacred thing because there is nothing more important than this quality in society.

In our drive for national recovery, we should expect national leaders to be credible. We can only be successful if we trust them and believe in them as credible—that is, if they are held in high esteem and seen as trustworthy. As Stephen Covey says, "If you want to be trusted, be trustworthy." The word trustworthy means that you always keep your word and tell the truth. We need to develop the ability to face the circumstances of our lives and see a situation as it is, not as we wish it could be. We can take control of our human and natural resources as well as our finances and not depend on foreign aids all the time. When our government spends more than its revenue generated or what is budgeted, we build a foundation of indebtedness.

Liberia is set to boom, and there is a fortune to be made. I discovered we are in the beginning stage on our road to financial independence, and this is the time that we gather around our leaders to help us make a difference in the community, and not just become preoccupied with what they are not doing. We should instead help our leaders do what they are supposed to do. Imagine a nation where opportunities are accessible to everyone regardless of socioeconomic background, a nation where we are given all the rights and responsibilities of democratic citizenship. In the words of French poet Victor Hugo, "Nothing is more powerful than an idea whose time has come."

The idea of having keys to national recovery is to craft an instrument for the present moment to successfully change the mistakes of the past—one that no political force can resist. For example, Mahatma Gandhi had an idea of India independence; others had the same idea. When the time was right for Mahatma's idea, not even the British Army could stop it. So those who resist the idea of change will either reinvent themselves or become irrelevant. We Liberians should voluntarily do things beyond ourselves if we want to achieve anything significant and bring change to this nation. We should not become hypersensitive to the opinions and possible destructive criticisms of other who do not wish this nation well. With all sincerity, God has allowed this book to be written to motivate and to inspire all Liberians and people in other nations that faced similar challenges to persist in carrying out efforts of national recovery despite the difficulties faced.

This book is a wakeup call because of what God is intended to do for the nation. There is a need to work with people from all occupations and not just to criticize and oppose them. It can be seen and understood that people in government are not infallible. Governments shall fall, but they must get up, dust themselves up, and make a change. Confucius said more than four thousand years ago, "Our greatest glory is not in never falling but in rising every time we fall." Also, Vince Lombardi said, "It's not whether you are knocked down but is whether you get up again." Sometimes leaders need to understand the difficult tasks in high offices, especially when it comes to economic recovery. Let not celebrate leaders for the positions they occupied, but what they achieved. We must not celebrate position; we must celebrate results.

When it comes to the choice of who will lead Liberia, Liberians must choose who they want, and they must be able to work with the leaders chosen by them. The effort of our leaders must also be respected, and we must do everything to keep the unity of this country, especially when we consider what happened to us in the past. Remember that economic recovery is a process and not just an event. It was a process that got us where we are today. Believe it or not, it will take a process to get us where we want to be. Again, it is not an event.

Economic recovery will be tedious, stressful, and strenuous; however, we must make a solemn commitment to stay alive with the process through the aid and the cooperation of the citizens. The sacred flame of national harmony, national republic, and national unity must not die. It is time for us as Liberians to take our destiny into our own hands. Commitment to little improvements in our nation will change our lives so profoundly that we will be astonished by what we will accomplish in the months and years ahead. Liberia is a very great nation. In the past, it served as a haven for a lot of people from different nations. We cannot be divided; it is now time for all Liberians to onboard the ship, "Sweet Liberia" to make a significant contribution. There is a statement by Niccolò Machiavelli that says, "If you want to control the people, separate the people, and you can rule them, divide them and you can conquer them." Let us come to understand that division will lead us to repeat the history of nonachievements.

Matthew 12:25 says, "Every Kingdom divided against itself is brought to desolation, and every city or home divided against itself shall not stand." The government takes all the blame for Liberia's problem, but I also believe that we can make a difference. I am so proud and blessed to be a Liberian. Fellow compatriots, let us keep wishing this nation the best and do what is right to bring God's blessings on it. Come on, Liberians! It is time to take your economy into your hands. You can make it! Rosalyn Carter said. "A leader takes people where they want to go, but a great leader takes people where they don't necessarily want to go but ought to be." We need leaders who will lead responsibly. Let us look at a portion of our national anthem for a while and reflect on the wording. "This glorious land of liberty shall long be ours." This should be our dream. We need to remember the kind of reputation we had just a few decades back. It takes a leader with a great vision to change the destiny of this nation. Great leaders have vision. It will take a great leader with a great vision to build the credibility of our nation around the world. Abraham Lincoln said, "Legitimate object of government is to do for a community of people whatever they need to have done but cannot do it all in their separate individual capacity." Sometimes it's not the system of our government that fails, but for the most part, it is those in government who fail the system.

We are talking about the keys to national recovery. If our government has the determination to achieve national recovery, then the history of corruption, failure, financial mismanagement, division, and like will not repeat itself. Now before the government draws up its plan for national recovery, it needs to know what has failed in the past. These are the lessons that history teaches. No doubt, Liberia is an emerging nation, but we can get there if we have the right leadership. Even though we have failed in the past, that failure should make us stronger and smarter. This is possible when we take the failures of the past, use them as tools in the present, to create a successful future. A piece of advice to our leaders is not to bury their failures; instead, be inspired by them. If you have read this far, then arrogance is not one of your problems. Arrogant people rarely read about the why; they feel they are the creators of the universe. By faith, I believe we can achieve this national goal.

Proverbs 29:2 (KJV) says "When the righteous are in authority, the people rejoice, but when the wicked rule, the people mourn." The word mourn or groan means "to feel or express sorrow or grief, showing deep sorrow or regret." The people will rejoice for the blessed effects on their good government. Indeed, when the righteous are in authority, the nation's wealth is properly managed, there is an increase in power (education) and wisdom, there is respect for the rule of laws, and God becomes the head of government. But when the wicked rule or when an ungodly man governs, the people mourn because of the oppressions and mischiefs they feel and because of the dreadful judgments of God, which they justly fear. As the saying goes, "actions speak louder than words." This scripture denotes our leaders are the captains of the nation's destiny, and the authority to rule justly is placed in their hands. According to Proverbs 29:18, paraphrased,

"Where there is no vision, the people perish," rather, cast off restraint, become ungovernable, will be ruined."

Sincerely speaking, I believed the time is coming when our leaders will not lead the Liberian people astray and cause them to mourn. With this said, leaders must be concerned with credibility because their integrity and reputation in the international community can be harmed. Being in leadership does not mean acting irresponsibly like some of our past leaders did. The offices of leadership required a responsible action. We expect our leaders to establish a godly foundation for the nation and to keep it from collapsing in the future. One of the marks of good leadership is to carefully deploy people or individuals of integrity in positions that will utilize their skills set. Good leadership is always thinking about what might be the highest and best use of time in fulfilling responsibilities. If you as a leader want the people you lead to become better, you must be a better leader to yourself by avoiding past mistakes. To avoid the history of "repeat" in Liberia, we must understand how to prevent wrong happenings and look at the historical perspective to find out the history of corruption, nonachievements, lack of transparency, issues of failure, and the lack of accountability to recover and thrust ahead.

CHAPTER 4

Vision for the Nation

We want to begin with God in this chapter. Psalm 89:19 says, "Once you spoke in vision to your godly ones, and said, 'I have given help to one who is mighty; I have exalted one chosen from the people." Vision has always been considered an important component in leadership. The nation cannot lead itself. We need a truly visionary leader. Visionary leaders have qualities that make them stand out from the rest of the crowd. Leadership begins when vision emerges. In this context, we need a vision for national recovery. Proverbs 29:18 says, "Where there is no vision, the people perish." Who are the people? The people are those who are led. They are the followers. Every nation needs a vision. By this I mean a concept of what the nation can achieve in God. Our vision is the ultimate achievement as a nation. We need such vision to motivate us, to give a definite and ultimate goal towards something to strive for, something to achieve, something for which it is worth sacrificing, a goal that will bring out the best in us as people.

Vision points toward the future (Proverbs 29:18). The writer of the book of Proverbs is talking about a prophetic vision (Consider the Hebrew word chazon, meaning "a revelation or Oracle vision.") When there is no vision, the people perished. One of my favorite translations says, "When there is no vision the people dwell carelessly," Unlawfully, and unrestrained; they live lives that lack purpose. The manifestation of no prophetic vision will give birth and nurture all that we see in this passage of scripture. Do you see the picture being presented to give us? Our nation has lacked vision and purpose for many years. Liberia has been like a ship without a rudder, and as a result, we dwell carelessly. We drift aimlessly through life from one independence celebration to another without any marks of true independence.

From a personal experience, there has been no sense of vision imparted to us in our schools since a child, no sense of individual and national destiny, no sense of purpose. As a servant of God called to the nation, I am calling on other servants of God to communicate their vision for the country with our people, instead of seeking political relevance and being religious fanatics. Leaders with a pure heart for this great nation who want to fulfill the purpose and leave a legacy for generations to follow must first define the vision for the country in clear and understandable words rather than in political jargon and clichés. One good place to start from is our Constitution. The Constitution gives us the right to do whatever is written and proper to keep the nation thriving. The president-elect must act responsibly as he or she steps into the most influential position to carry out the vision that was established by the founding fathers to recover nationally.

Our national leaders should watch over us; but instead, they prey upon us due to ignorance of our Constitutional rights. There has never been a well-defined vision for the nation regarding education. In our quest for recovery, we must prioritize education. Our leaders are quite willing to spend hundreds of millions of dollars on other things, but when you look around, you see that our public schools are in poor and delipidated condition and there are no textbooks for students. Our legislative branch should consider this very fundamental aspect of education and pass laws making education compulsory for every child. I read something about how a powerful man in the South of the United States wanted to prevent slaves from gaining an education; this indicates that people fully understand how empowering education can be. We are in the information age, so there is a need to address our educational shortcomings rather than just reciting political rhetoric. One thing we all must realize is that knowledge will always govern ignorance. Even God himself talks about this in Hosea 4:6, which says, "My people are destroyed for lack of knowledge." By remaining ignorant, we have opened ourselves up to slick politicians who use our rights to attain power. As you can see, some of the people in our society, who are easily led astray, are those with the poorest general education. And so those seeking political advantage always want to keep and maintain the status quo, preserving the uneducated people who can be easily manipulated.

Remember, we have a very poor history of placing no value on education. Our long-term independence and bilateral relationship with America gives us every reason to be one of the most educated people in the world. But because of our lack of educational vision, we drift aimlessly. People are looking for concrete answers to solve the problems of life; they have turned to astrologers, psychics, and so-called prophets. In Genesis 14:21, "the king of Sodom, though a Heathen prince, and perhaps a wicked man, yet had more regard to the persons of his subjects than to his own or their goods: the word for "goods" includes all the substance and possession of a man, gold, silver, cattle, and all movables." Previously in this passage, "The king of Sodom said to Abram, 'Give the people to me and take the goods for yourself.'" The king of Sodom placed value on the people; through the people, the economy of the nation expands.

When a nation is under the direction of a leader who has no vision, the result is confusion, disorder, rebellion, uncontrolled license, and at worst, anarchy. In its widest sense, prophecy denotes the revelation of God's will through his agents, who direct the course of events with supreme authority. The prophets were the instructors of the divine, standing as witnesses of the truth and power, teaching higher than mere human morality. The fatal effect of the absence of such revelation of God's will is stated to be confusion, disorder, and rebellion; the people fall into grievous excesses with no principles to restrain them.

In 1 Samuel 3, during the days of Eli, the priest, there was no open vision. Also, in Asa's days, when Israel had long been without a teaching priest in 2 Chronicles 15:3, when the impious Ahaz "made Judah naked," 2 Chronicles 28:19, or when they were destroyed by a lack of knowledge of divine things in Hosea 4:6. These are instances we can cite due to the lack vision. Thus, the importance of prophecy in regulating the life and religion of the people is fully acknowledged by the writers in Proverbs 29:12 "If a ruler pays attention to falsehood, all his ministers become wicked." Leaders have to be mindful of what accolade they received because they can easily be deceived by deceitful flatteries, misrepresentations, exaggerations, and falsehood of people who seek favor.

One of the keys to national recovery is genuine leadership. National recovery will be dependent on the leader's vision and dream for Liberia. It is the leader's vision that sets him or her apart from all others. With this clear-cut vision, to which our leaders will be wholeheartedly committed, it will ignite the first step to national recovery.

Next is "vision," the ability to project plans and hopes beyond the boundary of present circumstances. Albert Einstein said, "Problems cannot be solved by thinking within the framework in which the problems were created." We must begin to see Liberia in innovative ways. I believe people want to live, study, and practice in an organized environment. Our leaders need to provide the settings that will help people's natural drives and instincts for innovation to flourish, rather than to enforce curriculum development and other things that do not enhance (and in fact hinder) our intelligence. The leader who has a vision thinks and prepares for the future, while the leader who lacks vision lives only for the present. Liberians are perishing today because our leaders have no clear and exciting vision for the nation. Visionary leaders will take the time to think through and develop a clear picture of where they want the nation to be in six, twelve years or the future. The new leadership should have the ability to communicate the vision they have in such a way that others will buy in and eventually see the vision as theirs too. The vision must capture the possibilities of what we can accomplish, arouse participation, and motivate people to contribute their best.

The most compelling vision always aims at and describes values and mission rather than position. True leaders who want to build greatness in people will encourage them, instill confidence in them, and then help them perform at their best. Thus, this requires one to lead by example and do things differently. It is the leader's ability to imagine an ideal future well in advance, provide the blueprint and if possible take the lead that will enable ordinary men and women to rise to unprecedented levels in the nation, especially considering the impediments of modern life they must conquer.

When people have stakes in how their country is run, they are encouraged to contribute their best. President Thomas Jefferson said, "Every government degenerates when trusted to the rulers of the people alone. The people themselves, therefore, are its only safe depositories. And to render even them safe, their minds must be improved to a certain degree." Vision is the imaginary creation of the ideas leaders would like the people they lead to inhabit. I believe that from the very moment our leaders begin to develop an unclouded vision, they will start to be great leaders. They need to project themselves twenty to fifty years ahead, and they should always compare their activities against that vision and adjust their leadership activities appropriately. They are the molders and shapers of the destiny of the people. One good piece of advice for the new leadership must not only look at what conditions are necessary for a political gain, but also look at the underlying social conditions of what will make or break the nation in the long term. The leaders must examine our past as a nation to determine how we get to where we are today and decide how we are going to get from where we are to where they want us to be in the future under their leadership.

We need to do a trend analysis concerning Liberia as it exists today. A thorough investigation of the past and current situations can generate valuable insights into where we will be heading in the future. The situation analysis enables us to see the past, present, and future of the country. When we are clear about where we are coming from and where we are now and where we are going, we will become more determined about our national recovery. If we study the trend in our country over the past years and see that the trend is not satisfactory, then the job of the leader is to create a new plan and give us a course or path that points to a brighter future. This is all vision is about; it gives direction. Remember the old saying, "If you keep going in the same direction, you will end up where you are heading." A visionary leader will give direction to bring about national recovery. A vision is a clear picture of what a leader envisioned for his or her people. For example, Mahatma Gandhi had a vision of a free and independent India at a time when it was governed by the British. Also, in 1960, John F. Kennedy challenged the American people with his dream of putting an American on the moon by 1970. His vision immediately birthed the Apollo program. The president communicated his vision to the American people which the government and people committed themselves to the fulfillment of the vision. Another example, under the leadership of Lee Kuan Yaw, Singapore experienced such a radical change. In his book, From Third World to First World, Lee Kuna Yaw, the first prime minister of Singapore, recounts how his nation was transformed from a fragile democracy to a thriving economic marvel of Asia and the world. Nobody gave a chance to the survival of Singapore after it was expelled from Malaysia in 1965. Liberians have lost their dignity, glory, self-worth, self-value, a sense of purpose, senses of direction, sense of significance, and sense of independence. This national recovery could be a vision to recover all that we have lost. A vision like this is significant because it is the foundation of true leadership. Therefore, the effectiveness of the new and true leadership will depend on the clarity of the vision for national recovery. The vision for national recovery is not just for leadership acceptance, but it should be well embraced and encouraged by every citizen. It will be very refreshing and rewarding for leaders to act rather than react, to use the past only to gain insight into the present, to establish the direction for national recovery. If our leaders work toward this goal, through the cooperation of its people, by motivating them, it can be achieved. A leader with a vision will be dedicated to the cause of helping people find alternatives to life fulfillment. I believe there is an urgent need for a vision to transform our education system because our children's future is at stake. One could envision that when you have finished your course in six or twelve years, you (and every young person) could go to college and beyond regardless of your economic status. Thomas Jefferson is best known for drafting the Declaration of the Independence of America, but he also wrote prolifically and prophetically on education. He says, "If a nation expects to be ignorant and free, in a state of civilization, it expects what never was and never will be."

To recover, we should consider going back to the foundation of our Constitution because that is where our nation begins. From a constitutional perspective, our Constitution is like a vision. I refer to our Constitution as "constitutional vision." When someone assumes power as president, he or she swears an oath (the oath is written in article 53, section A.) Let us read the oath. "I do solemnly swear (or affirm) that I will faithfully execute the office of the president of the Republic of Liberia, and will do the best of my ability to preserve, protect, and defend the Constitution of the Republic of Liberia;" this is the key right. We need leaders who will keep us on track with our Constitution, but we see this aspect being abridged or overreached. Indeed, this is a national vision that was established by the founding fathers and was supposed to guide the nation into greatness by serving the purpose for which it was designed, ostensibly to reflect the aspirations of all Liberians. As part of our constitutional vision, we want to begin with our national flag. The flag was adopted to mark the nationality of the Republic of Liberia. It gives us an identity as a people to be distinguished from others. The flag was designed with the colors: red, white, and blue. The red stands for valor, the quality of being very brave, an honest and courageous way of behaving that people admired. Valor is honor plus dignity; it is gallantry and strength, great courage in the face of danger. The thesaurus defines it this way: "The quality of mind enabling one to face danger or hardship resolutely." I believe the word valor gives us a new definition of who we are to be.

Let us go back to the ancient paths and see where this word originated from in scripture, Jeremiah 6:16 says, "Stand by the roads, and look, and ask for the ancient paths." Judges 6:12 says, "And the angel of the Lord appeared to him, and said to him, 'The Lord is with you, you mighty man of valor." indeed, this is the road to national recovery that will prepare the nation for greatness. The meaning of the word valor has a lot to do with the context of the statement. "To understand what the angel meant we need to look at the framework of the situation when the angel came to Gideon. Israel was given over to the Midianites because they disobeyed God. They cried out, and God answered their call. Gideon was threshing wheat in the wine press to hide from the Midianites when the angel met him." (The Ancient Path, 2013). Can you see some parallels to our situation? Judges 6:13 says, "O my Lord if the Lord is with us, why then has all this happened to us?" This was Gideon's question, and this is also the question many Liberians ask. "If Liberia was established on Christian principles, why then is all of this happening to us?" When we blame God for our situation, it becomes difficult to have insight into the future by faith. If we do not have confidence in God, we will not have self-confidence because an incorrect view of ourselves is a wrong view of God. We are made in his image. It is good to have a biblical, academic, and experiential knowledge of God. If we study the Word of God, then just like Gideon, we will come to understand that it is our disobedience that brought about the situation we are in today and not God's inability to solve our problems.

Moreover, as John Wooden said, "the greatest failure of all is the failure to act when action is needed." It is time to apply our acts of valor to reclaim the national valor we have lost. In this process of the vision for national recovery, we can become a force of valor. Let us define the word process to gain an understanding of how this will work. A process is a repeatable and organized set of actions performed to produce a result of value. Let us expand on this. Leaders are to organize and perform actions to achieve the expected results. Wow! May the Lord help us. The process of valor and commitment produce valor. Webster's Dictionary says valor is "strength of mind or spirit that enables a man to encounter danger with firmness; personal bravery; heroism." Learning the truth about our nation can be shocking at times, but it is the truth that brings deliverance (John 8:32). I believe that we can be men and women of valor in the true spirit and context of this word. It will transcend all other areas of our lives. Understanding the true meaning of the word valor brings hope because God's plan for Liberia cannot be thwarted once we live with the spirit of valor. God still works and controls random situations like ours. By faith, we can take a God-centered approach to save Liberia and give it a new beginning and purpose. Somewhere along the line, we lost direction, but there is a way out, and the only way is God's way. "There is a way which seems right to a man (to a nation), but its end is the way of destruction." (Proverbs 16:25). This is where we are today, but in God's eyes, it does not matter where we are as a nation. He is still reaching out to people like you and me to use. I challenge you today before you finish reading this book to bring deliverance to your nation with what God has birthed in you.

Throughout the Bible, whenever God got ready to deliver the nation of Israel, He picked men of valor, not the weakest person in the family. For example, and the angel of the Lord appeared to you, put your name there, and said, "God is saying something to you. The Lord is with you, you mighty man of valor." And the Lord turned to him and said, "Go in this might of yours and deliver Israel from the hand of Midian. Have I not sent you?" God is turning and pointing to you as a reader and saying, Mighty men and women of valor, go and deliver Liberia from the hands of the enemies of progress, greedy and corrupt people who get to the place of leadership just to plunder and devastate the land.

To give you a picture of what is happening in Liberia, we need to go a little further. Judges 6:4–7 says, "And they encamped against them, and destroyed the increase of the earth, till thou come unto Gaza, and left no sustenance for Israel, neither sheep, nor ox, nor ass. For they came up with their cattle and their tents, and came as grasshoppers for multitude; for both they and their camels were without number: and they entered into the land to destroy it. And Israel was greatly impoverished because of the Midianites; and the children of Israel cried unto the Lord because of the Midianites," friends, this is our mission. Wherever you see Israel in these passages, insert Liberia. In Numbers 13 and 14, the leaders of the tribes looked at the adversity and problems that were confronting them, and they saw the weakness that was inside of them. Instead of being assets, they became obstacles. God has sent the answer to you, the reader. The Lord is perfectly able to raise his instrument to carry out his purpose. I urge you to come on the Lord's side, the winning side. Exodus 32:25–26 says, "Now when Moses saw that the people were out of control … For Aaron had let them get out of control to be a derision among their enemies: then Moses stood in the gate of the camp and said, whoever is for the LORD" This is exactly what happens when leaders do not have control of themselves as shown in the passage. God said the people were out of control because Aaron had let them get out of control; thus, the result was derision. This is when people make fun of you, laughing, and acting as if you are worthless. This is what happened to the children of Israel when Aaron lost control of his leadership, and things got out of control. This is what needs to be changed in Liberia, but change does not come from the mob or the bottom; it comes from the head—leaders who have high standards and truly stand for the standards they set.

This is what God is saying. He has chosen you from among the crowd to help you lead, to give you a big picture for the nation and imprint the vision into others. Webster's Dictionary defines leadership as the power or ability to lead other people. The first question an aspiring leader should ask himself or herself is this: "What is my view of leadership and the vision I have?" You should be ready to put the nation and your mission first, to lead the people but not for your selfish aims. Be a leader who will maintain the nation's trust through oversight and accountability. Habakkuk 2:2–3(AMP) says, "And the Lord answered me and said, Write the vision and engrave it so plainly upon tablets that everyone who passes may [be able to] read [it easily and quickly] as he hastens by. For the vision is yet for an appointed time and it hastens to the end [fulfillment]; it will not deceive or disappoint, though it tarries, [earnestly] wait for it because it will surely come to pass." Vision brings answers.

The vision must be written for people to see. And we must carry it out. We have seen those who come to the place of leadership in our nation come with no vision, how can the people run without a written vision. The previous passage says it will not deceive, meaning the people are deceived because the leaders come with no vision. The New Living Translation says, "Then the Lord said to me, write my answer plainly on tablets so that a runner can carry the correct message to others." This means the right message has to be plainly written before it can be carried out. Niccolò Machiavelli says, "It is just as difficult and dangerous to try to free people who want to remain servile as it is to enslave people who want to remain free." This is our predicament as Liberians. Do we want to be free or remain servile?

If we can only go back to our national flag and study the meaning of the three colors, we will appreciate ourselves and realize that we are a vital link to the future generations. We have a legacy worth preserving and a future worth fighting for. Our constitutional vision gives us values that we should uphold. It lays the foundation for the rules that we are expected to adhere to, but the spirit of the constitutional vision has been tampered with and misinterpreted. That is why Liberia is now experiencing many social disorders, anarchy, and complex problems.

Liberians are yearning for a true patriot. The word root of Patriot in Latin is pater, meaning "father." John Q Moron said, Originally, a patriot was someone who loves their country and supports it, but won't blindly follow whatever their country's government does. These days, it is synonymous with Nationalist, which is someone who blindly follows whatever his country's government does, and lacks his own ability to think and reason for himself." A true patriot is someone who loves his country enough to speak up when he sees something that needs to be changed, not someone who blindly assumes that their government knows best and is always right no matter what. D. Shiznit said, "A patriot loves his country to the extent that he will work to change it or point out what his country's government is doing wrong." Also, DaVxOr said, "A true patriot in the sense of the word that is a visionary will wish to change the government to run the way the Constitution describes it should, someone who will inspire and motivate us to set national goals and instilled in us confidence and the spirit to achieve them." But in our postwar country today, Liberians tend to view politicians as those who are well-connected and eloquent, people we think have the money to influence elections. We always choose our leaders based on their outward appearances, but many of them are like wolves in sheep's clothing.

Our choice of a leader should not be based on what that leader appears to be. The prophet Samuel was a human being just like us. Even with all his prophetic sightings, he was deceived by the outward appearance of David's brothers, but God corrected him. I Samuel 16:7, "But the Lord said to Samuel, "Do not look on his appearance or on the height of his stature, because I have rejected him. For the Lord sees not as man sees: man looks on the outward appearance, but the Lord looks on the heart." We should be mindful this time about the person we elect to lead and not just for ourselves as we did in the past, but for the future of our nation. Hosea 8:4 says, "They set up kings without my consent; they choose princes without my approval." Further, I Corinthians 1:26–27 says, "For you see your calling, brethren, that not many wise according to the flesh, not many mighty, not many noble, are called. But God has chosen the foolish things of the world to put to shame the wise, and God has chosen the weak things of the world to put to shame the things which are mighty;"

Many people desired to be leaders, some for noble purposes, some for self-serving reasons, and some have a desire to serve God's purpose. The election was evident with Old Testament leaders as well. To David, God says, "I took you from the pasture, from following the sheep, that you should be leader over my people Israel" (1 Chronicles 17:7). Indeed, prophets were chosen people who anointed all the legitimate kings of Israel. This is the time for the most crucial decision in the nation, and our mission is not to elect leaders without vision and put them in power. On the contrary, our mission is to discern whom God has chosen to be a leader and to ratify or recognize that choice. We should choose a leader who will rise above personal and individual perspective to take a national view. Even our national anthem details a vision and a mission that our leaders should be truly dedicated and devoted to without just seeking their glory. We want a leader who will be genuinely interested in the welfare of the Liberian people. Where there's no vision, the people dwell carelessly, unrestrained, drifting through life aimlessly and unlawfully. Yes, Liberians needs visionary leaders. We do not need politicians who use senseless rhetoric to inspire the support of the people, but people with vision, direction, and strength to reach the national goal.

The purpose of this book is to give us a renewed focus. Let us come to the second color in our national flag and its meaning. The white symbolizes purity. Matthew 5:8 (AMP) says, "Blessed are the pure in heart for they shall see God." This refers to someone with a heart that is unmixed in devotion and motivation—pure motives from a pure heart. To be pure in body is good, but to be pure in heart is the best of all because it takes care of both the internal and the external. If we are pure in our hearts, we will be pure inside out. To be pure in the heart means to be pure from the inside out. The word purity describes the kind of people we should be from God's point of view. In Matthew 23, we see Jesus's scathing pronouncement against the external purity as practiced by the Pharisees. We need to picture ourselves in what Jesus was saying to the Pharisees for us to recover nationally. Woe to you, scribes and Pharisees, hypocrites! For "you clean the outside of the cup and of the dish, but inside they are full of robbery and self-indulgence." This is Liberia's condition. Max Lucado, a Christian author on the topic, says that pure heart, says "clean the refinery, and the result will be a pure product. We usually reverse the order. We try to change the inside by altering the outside" Exodus23:8 says, "You shall not take a bribe, for a bribe blinds the clear-sighted and subverts the cause of the just." Someone put it this way: "Take no bribe, for a bribe makes you ignore things you might see clearly." "A bribe makes even a righteous person twist the truth. "Exodus 23:8. Here's the solution to our problem. Ezekiel 14:6, says, "Therefore, say to the house of Israel" (says to the nation Liberia) — "Thus says the Lord God, 'Repent and turn away from your idols and turn your faces away from all your abominations.'" If the white in our national flag symbolizes purity, then we need national repentance and deliverance for national recovery.

Thou shalt take no gift (i.e., no bribe). Bribery has always been rife in Liberia, and the pure administration of justice is almost unknown. This is one of the areas that have blinded us over the years. Let us understand why we need to repent. A bribe is money or favor given or promised to influence the judgment or conduct of a person in a trusted position. Bribery is a blinding influence upon wisdom and discernment. It also perverts the words of those who would be righteous in the sight of God. Bribery is the act of taking or receiving something with the intention of influencing the recipient in some way that is favorable to the party providing the bribe. If this is you, you cannot pledge allegiance to the national flag. It requires a heart of purity, something you do not possess.

Finally, the third color: blue in the national flag represents fidelity. These are some of the constitutional visions the founding fathers wanted us to represent whenever the flag is raised and waved—valor, purity, and fidelity. Let us deal with the word fidelity. Merriam-Webster's Dictionary defines it as "allegiance, fealty, piety, loyalty, and devotion." Piety means "faithfulness to something to which pledge or duty bind one, the fidelity owed by a subject or citizen to a sovereign or government." According to these definitions, a pledge binds us. "I pledge allegiance to the flag of Liberia and to the republic for which it stands, one nation, indivisible with liberty and justice for all." That is the key for the new visionary leaders.

Again, let us look at the word allegiance and see what our responsibility is. Our responsibility is to be loyal to a cause, to a nation, or to a leader. This is what we have neglected. When a nation stumbles on the roots of its problems, all the people get as a solution is a feeble and temporary answer. It is like dealing with a symptom and not the disease. Now we want to understand exactly what our founding fathers' plan for this great nation was and exactly what the pledge of allegiance means to each of us. Many of us do not even know what we are saying when we recite the pledge of allegiance. So, we want to break it down to understand it line by line and word for word. According to UShistory.org, the pledge "I" refers to ownership. A person speaking is referring to him or herself when the individual says "I." It is personal. It is a solemn promise or agreement to do or refrain from doing something. The person speaking is promising or agreeing to what he or she is saying. Allegiance refers to loyalty, dedication, devotion, fidelity, honor, and obedience. "To" is a preposition used to express motion or direction toward a noun (person, place, or thing) rather than any motion or direction away from a noun. "The flag" is a piece of cloth of various shapes with a combination of colors and designs, and it is customarily attached on one edge to a pole or cord. Flags represent nations, states, or organizations.

The Republic of Liberia is an area of land governed as a republic. It is in West Africa, and it formed when fifteen individual counties together as one. Liberia as a republic was primarily founded by the American Colonization Society (ACS), a group of white Americans, including some slaveholders, who had what certainly can be described as mixed motives. They later called themselves Americo-Liberians. Liberia was founded in 1822 as a settlement of freed slaves from the United States, and it was proclaimed independent in 1847. It was never officially colonized, but it became a sphere of influence and interest for the United States. A republic is a form of government in which the powers of sovereignty are authorized by and entrusted to the people and executed by the people either directly or through representatives chosen by the people to whom those powers are specially appointed. The phrase "for which it stands," the position or opinion of someone, one - single, alone or solitary. Nation, a country with its government. Indivisible - impenetrable, inseparable, joined, permanent, unbreakable, unified, indissoluble; with, accompanying. Including liberty and freedom, independence; and, in addition to; justice, lawfulness, fairness, honesty, integrity; for, as long as (it is); all, entire, total, complete. From following the pledge, lots of things have broken down. It makes perfect sense to start all over again to achieve national recovery; we have to understand our pledge of allegiance. It is a sad thing seeing this great nation fall apart. We should do everything within our power to protect and fight for the sweet Liberia that God has so blessed us with and not be a part of its destruction.

Abraham Lincoln said, "America will never be destroyed from the outside. If we falter and lose our freedoms, it will be because we destroyed ourselves." He also warned that mobs or people who disrespected American laws and courts could destroy the United States. This is exactly what has happened to us as Liberians. May this book help us take back what we have lost.

Officials of the government embezzled state funds for their use with no disciplinary system under which they could be punished. They violated ethical standards, and the laws and the court system were compromised and broken down with impunity. Life becomes impoverished, and depredation and devastation follow. Thomas Jefferson said, "No nation is permitted to live in ignorance with impunity."

We are in a movement of political maneuvering and manipulation, which significantly hurts us as people. We want a true leader who will bring about transformative change and make Liberia a great nation, a leader who will demonstrate strong moral values, one imbued with high ethical standards. Yes, we want that the visionary leader for our nation, a person through whom there will be a fair and equitable distribution of wealth. The idea of our nation expressed in our Constitution, so we need a visionary constitutional leader who will make us feel that being Liberian is not a disgrace but an honor. Please do not forget that your vision brands you. We need a visionary leader who will bring his or her vision and present the future of Liberia to us.

Vision brings victory. We keep failing because of our lack of vision. God says again, "Where there's no vision the people perish." They fail. There is no victory. Vision brings better education, fulfillment, and accomplishment. Where there is no vision, creativity and innovation are not rewarded. A nation without a vision is a nation without a future, and a nation without a future will always return to its past because there is nothing to look forward to. That is why we celebrate William Tubman's birthday, characterized by high levels of pleasure and immorality that have caused us to experience damaging effects. Paul says, "It's this way I press on toward the goal for the prize of the upward calling of God in Christ Jesus" (Philippians 3:14). When there is a vision, you see how to go onward and upward, not backward. Paul also talked about goals. In the vision for the nation, we must set goals.

There is a big error in our pledge: we omitted God from it, as the Americans did originally, only to insert "under God" later. We recite our pledge this way: "I pledge allegiance to the flag of Liberia and to the Republic for which it stands one nation indivisible with liberty and justice for all." We need to go back and review our constitutional vision and retrace our steps to see whether we are directly attached to the mission of the constitutional vision. If not, we can either redefine our mission or redirect our steps.

CHAPTER 5

Enemies of Progress

An old African proverb says, "when there is no enemy within, the enemies outside cannot hurt you." The enemy of progress is an individual who undermines the growth and development of anything without providing any positive alternatives. Thus, the enemy of progress as it pertains to Liberian is an individual who does everything to undermine the growth, development, and integrity of the nation without providing any solutions.

The first enemy of progress - those who get away with evil in the nation in such as corruption, embezzlement, and others. Those public servants who have stolen millions in taxpayers funds and gone with impunity can be branded as enemies of progress because they committed these acts against the society. There are people within the government who do things that are contradictory to the principles embodied in the Constitution.

The second enemy of progress - those who violate the oath of office. For instance, people swearing to the oath of office are obligated to stand for what they swore.

The oath of office for every civil servant and military officer of the Republic of Liberia requires that the individual "support and defend the Constitution of the Republic of Liberia against all enemies: foreign and domestic." As cited in the Constitution,

> Schedule 1. "This Schedule shall form and be an integral part of this Constitution and shall have the same force as any other provision thereof." Schedule 2. All public officials and employees, whether elected appointed,

> holding office of public trust, shall subscribe to a solemn oath or affirmation as follows: "I, do solemnly swear (affirm) that I will support, uphold, protect, and defend the Constitution and laws of the Republic of Liberia, bear true faith and allegiance to the Republic, and will faithfully, conscientiously, and impartially discharge the duties and functions of the office to the best of my ability. So help me God.

Many people have taken such an oath, but only a few have tried to live up to it. Because of our citizenship as Liberians, we are responsible for maintaining the integrity of the Constitution. An oath is an act of calling upon God as a witness to what one says, thereby treating it as sacred. Violation of an oath or vow is an offense against God. Therefore, People who took oaths in this nation often abused them, swearing by things they will in no form fulfill which is unaccepted to God. God himself set an example of taken an oath in Deuteronomy 9:5, "It is not because of your righteousness or your integrity that you are going in to take possession of their land; but on account of the wickedness of these nations, the LORD your God will drive them out before you, to accomplish what he swore to your fathers, to Abraham, Isaac, and Jacob." The issue of vow or oath is reinforced in Matthew 5:33, "Again you have heard that the ancients were told, 'You shall not make false vows, but shall fulfill your vows to the LORD." I Peter 5:8 says, "Be of sober spirit, be on the alert. Your adversary, the devil, prowls around like a roaring lion, seeking someone to devour." In this context, we can consider an adversary as someone who was elected and has taken the oath to serve in government but became corrupt and sabotaged the nation in some way. These adversaries embraced legal positivism, sue for nihilistic libertinism, and seek ways to avoid the consequences of their actions.

The third enemy of progress - those who fall in the Social strain theory developed by a famed American sociologist named Robert K. Merton. He wrote in his research "that social structures within society may pressure citizens to commit crimes." Systems of society affect the perception and needs of its people. Many in government today have been so badly influenced by the corrupt system that they have form coalitions to overwhelm the society with the sheer force of people who defend them because of social strain. Many leaders have taken public offices with good intention but allowed the corrupt system to thwart their plans for evil.

The fourth enemy of progress is treachery which can be seen in Psalm 119:158, "I behold the Treacherous and loathe them because they do not keep your word." Moreover, Proverbs 2:22 says, "But the wicked will be cut-off from the land and the treacherous will be uprooted from it." Proverbs 13:15 says, "Good understanding produces favor, but the way of the treacherous is hard." When treacherous people lead a nation, things get very hard. Treachery, behavior or an action in which certain people betray their country or betray a person who trusts them." The Webster's Revised Unabridged Dictionary defines it as "the violation of allegiance or faith and confidence. "It is an act of perfidy or treason. These different definitions are for clarity, to give us a picture of the real enemy of progress in the nation. Since independence, the Liberian people have elected several leaders but almost all if not, everyone has let the people down by betraying their trust. The noun treachery comes from the old French word trechier, which means "to cheat." Many corrupt governments or dictators have been accused of treachery, deceiving the people and abusing their trust. Greed is a common cause of treachery; and with the promise of wealth, people can be tempted to betray their own countries. Thomas Jefferson said, "Injustice in government undermines the foundations of a society." A nation, therefore, must take measures to encourage its members along the paths of justice and morality. The judicial system was established so that people could remedy many injustices and prosecute individuals who stand as enemies of progress. Several decades ago J. Reuben Clark spoke about the need for a solid support of the Constitution. He said,

> God provided that in this land of liberty, our political allegiance shall run not to individuals, that is, to government officials, no matter how great or how small they may be. Under His plan, our allegiance and the only allegiance we owe as citizens or denizens of the United States, runs to our inspired Constitution which God himself set up. So, runs the oath of office of those who participate in government. A certain loyalty we do owe to

> the office which a man holds, but even here we owe just by reason of our citizenship, no loyalty to the man himself. In other countries it is to the individual that allegiance runs. This principle of allegiance to the Constitution is basic to our freedom. It is one of the great principles that distinguishes this "land of liberty" from other countries.

The fifth enemy of progress - those who compromise the truth. The Lord God says in Psalm 11:3, "If the foundations are destroyed, what can the righteous do?" Today church leaders are compromising the pure gospel of God's grace and mingling it with the idols of secular religion. There are lots of churches today in our society compromising the gospel by joining with groups who claim to believe it. According to our history, as a nation gained independence in 1847, we were supposed to represent the continent of Africa. A lone, five-pointed star in the center of a blue field in our flag depicted the only independent republic in Africa at that time.

The sixth enemy of progress is the Crippling mentality. A crippling mindset will create a crippling condition or a crippling environment. Let us look at the story of the Crippled man being carried in Acts 3 at the Gate Beautiful. If you carefully read the story, you will find the same picture in our nation which describes both the spiritual and physical conditions of Liberia. Crippled means that you are unable to do certain things others can do in a way that is normal. You also can define the crippling condition as being reduced in physical or mental capacity to the degree that is sufficiently less than societal norms, thus impairing daily living and affecting national progress. We are crippled in mentality and advancement, unable to catch up with the fast development of other nations. The crippled man sits at the beautiful gate, looks at its beauty, and just begs for alms. In this story, God is pointing to us regarding the nation that is always asking and wanting to be helped; thereby compromising our destiny. We are at the gate beautiful, surrounded by vast natural resources that we can utilize; instead, we are waiting for someone to come and help us. There is a grave need to rise to the challenges our nation faces and move from the position of handout to stand out. Let this be clear! It is not wrong to be helped, but if you are solely depended upon the aid of others, so your growth and development will.

As a famous saying goes, "Give a Man a Fish, and You Feed Him for a Day. Teach a Man To Fish, and You Feed Him for a Lifetime." Although this is seen from the physical, it has a spiritual significance to our lives. It is the spiritual atmosphere that governs a person's life and determines what happens to that individual. Therefore, Recovery takes place first in the unseen spiritual realm before it manifests in the natural realm. Please read 1 Samuel 30:8. In that passage, King David inquired from the spiritual realm and received instructions on the God-ordained strategy for recovery. Hence, this is meant to enable the sons and daughters of Liberia to look both into the spiritual and natural conditions we faced to gain an understanding of the circumstances perpetuating this crippling condition.

The seventh enemy of progress – those in secret society. Being a member of a secret society like the Freemasons and other local secret societies, you are an enemy of God. Exodus 20:3 says, "You shall have no other god before Me." Because these people are enemies of God, that is what makes them the enemy of progress in the land. There is a solution, and that is to repent. Acts 26:20 says, "But kept declaring both to those of Damascus first, and also at Jerusalem and throughout all the region of Judea, and even to the Gentiles, that they should repent and turn to God, performing deeds appropriate to repentance." II Kings 17:41 gives us an insight into these various societies: "So while these nations feared the Lord, they also served their idols; their children likewise and their grandchildren, as their fathers did, so they do to this day."

The truth is God knew we would come to this day of realization. Being a part of different secret societies was something passed onto us. For instance, when daily horoscope emerged as a journalistic feature in the country, the early presentations quickly appealed to a receptive public sentiment, and the horoscope column has become a regular aspect of tabloid and syndicated newspapers ever since. Since then, the zodiac signs have been a significant influence on people's lives.

What does the Bible say about zodiac signs? Micah 5:12 says, "And I will cut off sorceries from your hand, and you shall have no more tellers of fortunes." John 14:6 says, "Jesus said to him, 'I AM the way, and the truth, and the life, No one comes to the Father except through Me.'" II Peter1:21 says, "For no prophecy was ever produced by the will of man, but men spoke from God as they were carried along by the Holy

Spirit." Jeremiah10:2 says, "Thus says the Lord, 'Learn not the way of the nations, nor be dismayed at the signs of the heavens because the nations are dismayed at them." From these passages of scripture, you can see that the indulgence in such act of secret society brought a gloomy situation upon us.

Let us look at the beliefs of Freemasons; those beliefs are ungodly and occultic. What we are saying based on various studies is this: at its core, Freemason is not a Christian organization. There are many Christians who have left Freemasonry after discovering what it is truly about. People who claimed to be Christian and are part of Freemasonry or other secret societies are walking to profound error and confusion. We contend that this is because they do not truly understand freemasonry or the bible they professed to believe. The bible speaks profoundly on the issue of secret society. Creating secret code words or handshakes are all acts of secrecy that the Bible frown upon. Freemasons, Eastern Star, and other similar secret organizations appear to be harmless in their fellowship gatherings. Many of them appear to promote belief in God; however, upon closer examination, you can discover that a person only needs to believe in a supreme being which could be the gods of Islam, Hinduism, or any other world religion.

The following compares what the Bible says about the official position of a secret society or an ungodly organization. The unbiblical and anti-Christian beliefs and practices of this organization are partially hidden beneath an outward appearance of a compatibility with the Christian faith. When a Christian takes the oath of Freemasonry, for example, he or she swears to the following doctrines that man's good works can gain salvation. Also, that Jesus is just one of many equal Reverends and prophets about whom they will remain silent in their lodge, not talking about Christ. They are approaching the lodge in spiritual darkness and ignorance. When the Bible says Christians are already in the light; the light of the Word of Jesus Christ indwells them. By demanding that Christians take the Masonic oath, Masonry leads Christians into blasphemy and taking the name of the Lord in vain. Exodus 20:7 says, "You shall not take the name of the Lord your God in vain." The Lord will not leave him unpunished who takes his name in vain.

The Word dismayed that the prophet Jeremiah used in the previous scripture quoted, is defined like this: "to be shattered, be broken, cracked, beat down." Because of our constant disobedience, we have developed a deviant behavior, criminal and noncriminal activities. Our lawmakers are involved in such activities. A lawmaker cannot be a law breaker at the same time. Secret society breaks down the spiritual fabrics of the nation although the society activities may appear to be physically helpful. Thus, the practices of secret society make us a deviant nation. Deviance is any behavior that veers away from social norms and what is taught. Primary deviance refers to the initial act of a person's negative behavior. If the person continues to veer away from acceptable behavior, then their actions are titled secondary deviance. Isaiah7:8 says, "For the head of Aram is Damascus and the head of Damascus is Rezin." (Now within another sixty-five years, Ephraim will be shattered, and it will no longer have a people.) Isaiah 8:9 says, "Be broken, O peoples, and shattered; and give ear, all remote places of the earth. Gird yourselves, yet be shattered; Gird yourselves, yet be shattered." To be shattered means to break something into pieces as with a blow, to damage as by breaking or crushing. It also means to impair, destroy, or weaken. We have been labeled as a nation in defiance to God and the enemy of progress (EOP) to our nation because of our involvement in the act of secret society.

The Bible's view on human nature and sin is that all humans are born with a sinful nature and are totally depraved and need a Savior from sin (Romans 3:23; 5:12; Psalm 51:5; Ephesians 2:1). The Bible denies that because of the fall, humanity has within itself the capacity for moral perfection (1 John 1:8–10; Romans 1:18–25). We are off track here. God only reveals to us how people become enemies of progress in a nation. Let's see the Freemason's view. Through symbols and emblems, Freemasons teach that "man is not sinful but just rude and imperfect by nature." Human beings can improve their character and behavior in many ways, including acts of charity, moral living, and voluntary performance of civic duty. Humanity can move from imperfection toward total perfection. Moral and spiritual perfection lies within men and women. We cannot believe in God and at the same time swear secret oaths to other things that invoke the wrath of God upon us. Jesus said in John 8:32, "Ye shall know the truth, and the truth shall make you free."

In his farewell address to the elders at Ephesus, Paul warned them to be on guard because savage wolves would attack the flock. Acts 20:26–31 says.

> Therefore, I testify to you this day that I am innocent of the blood of all men, for I did not shrink from declaring to you the whole purpose of God, be on guard for yourselves and for all the flock, among which the Holy Spirit has made you overseers, to shepherd the church of God which he purchased with his own blood, that after my departure savage wolves will come in among you, not sparing the flock: and from among your own selves men will arise, to draw away the disciples after them, therefore, be on the alert, remembering that night and day for a period of three years I did not cease to admonish each one with tears.

This is the purpose of this book—to open our eyes to the realities that surround us. Masons are highly committed not to divulge the truth about their philosophy for many reasons known to them. First, they have taken oaths to keep such information confidential. First Peter 5:8 says, "Be of sober spirit, be on the alert, your adversary [enemy] the devil, prowls around like a roaring lion, seeking someone to devour." I pray that after reading this book, you will not be that person. Proverbs 16:7 says, "When the Lord takes pleasure in anyone's way, he causes their enemies to make peace with them." Acts 26:18 says, "To open their eyes so that they may turn from darkness to light and from the dominion of Satan to God, that they may receive forgiveness of sins and an inheritance among those who have been sanctified by faith."

There is a labeling theory developed by Frank Tannenbaum that says how the self-identity and behavior of individuals may be determined or influenced. Our behavior as a nation has become a stigma. A stigma is defined as a powerfully negative label that changes a person's self-concept and social identity. This describes our leaders. This is a sad condition as a nation established on Christian principles. We expect representatives and individuals such as police officers and judges to make more biblically and godly respected judgments. The rule of law must govern any nation that wants to progress. Social roles are necessary for the governing and functioning of any society. For example, we expect revenue collectors to adhere to certain fixed rules about how they do their job.

How do you perceive yourself and your relationship with society? As Galatians 5:14 says, "For the whole Law is fulfilled in one word in the statement, 'You shall love your neighbor as yourself.'" Liberians do not have financial problems. What we have is a trust problem. The rise and fall and the turning point of Liberia come at a very crucial time in the nation's history. To achieve national recovery, we must value the rule of law because it is important to the survival and advancement of our nation and not a secret society."

CHAPTER 6

Areas of Financial Failure

"Government failure is a situation where government intervention in the economy to correct a market failure creates inefficiency and leads to a misallocation of scarce resources;" (Government Failure, Economics online) which includes government subsidies, taxation on goods and service, and fix prices. There are several areas for government failure, but this chapter discusses five areas of great concern.

The first area: Lack of incentives - people want to be motivated and appreciated for what they do and not just being paid for what they do. If a government does not put into place programs or measures that will award, appreciate, and motivate people, the performance of the people will be at an average level, or they will underperform because there is nothing to drive their innovation, energy levels, and make them feel a part of what they do. Over the years of existence, the government of Liberia has not instituted measures or programs that will boost the performance levels of its citizenry. This inhuman act of the government has birthed corruption, embezzlement, underperformance, and underdevelopment to the nation. For example, the national police, considering the high risks involved in their job, there must program in place that will award their hard work, not just a paycheck.

The second area: The lack of sufficient and relevant information. "Politicians may have inadequate information about the type of service to provide; they may not be experts in their department, but concentrate on their political ideology." If we are to thoroughly look at the activities of most politicians in our nation, not many of them can sense and meet the needs that are prevalence in the country because their political ideologies consume them. Many of our politicians lived in communities where there are serious needs to be met, but they blatantly ignore the realities of the situations because of their political agenda and egotism.

The third area: Political inference. The Government takes the "short term view rather than considering long term effects" on the major endeavors she undertakes such as infrastructure development, entrepreneurship development, educational development, healthcare delivery system and the list goes on. The conflict between political and economic objectives paved the way for the destruction of Liberia's emerging economy. The leaders' economic policy of our nation is based on a "Get Rich Quick" mentality which has made it difficult to institute sustainable financial rules and regulations. Sir Winston Churchill once said, "The road to hell is paved with good intentions." Cambridge Dictionary emphasizes "that you must not simply intend to behave well, but you must act according to your intentions because you will have problems or be punished if you do not." "Promises and plans must be put into action, or else they are useless."

I believe history reflects that the short-term benefits given to the generations from the 1920s and 1930s were provided at the expense of future generations. Liberia's abundant natural resources include diamonds, gold, iron ore, rubber, and timber. From the 1920s, Liberia became dependent on the exploitation of natural resources, particularly the rubber industry and the Firestone company. This period provided the impetus that solidified the Liberian government's role as the chief economic architect during said time. The country economic survival needed strong leadership, but Liberians had no such mentality in that era or did our elected officials. During those periods, the country was suffering in tumultuous times, but because of the surpluses, the country's economy was also moving on.

Majority of the government officials exhibited high levels of corruption, limiting government effectiveness. They were mortgaging future generations to feed their indulgences, and this made the economy suffer significantly. Foreigners mostly controlled the business sector, mainly people of Lebanese and Indian descent who sneaked millions of dollars out of the country. There was no openness and transparency. The lack of transparency and integrity, which are essential elements, did not help us resolve the issues of corruption. Officials privatized and mismanaged public funds, and there were no laws or guidelines of handling finances. The violations of fiduciary duties of trustees and unequal access to the benefits of natural resources created societal rifts as the government began to borrow and plunge us into huge debt. Proverbs 22:7 says, "The rich rules over the poor, and the borrower becomes the lender's slave." It is why are we experiencing financial failure. The corruption that is so systemic is also of the result of deficit spending. Williams Vickrey states that "deficit spending is the amount by which spending exceeds revenue over a particular period." He further said, "Deficits are considered to represent sinful profligate spending at the expense of future generations who will be left with a smaller endowment of invested capital." Proverbs 22:7 is a scriptural warning about borrowing money. God calls Christians to keep out of debt altogether. "Owe no man anything, but to love one another" (Romans 13:8). Borrowing constitutes a judgment of God. Do you see the picture? "In the Old Testament, borrowing was evidence that the people of Israel were facing God's judgment." Borrowing results in bondage to creditors. The very nature of going in debt is entanglement. The Hebrew words for borrow mean "to twine to unite, to borrow (as a form of obligation)" (lavah) and figuratively "to entangle" (abat). Scripture warns that "the borrower is a servant to the lender."

Because of borrowing, Liberia's debt is always paid at the cost of its people's survival. The government has consumed her asset base by transferring her economy to foreigners without regulation that will benefit the Liberian people. For national recovery to be achieved, the government must build trust with the people. Moreover, the economy will live or die based on the public's confidence in the government; If trust is lost, the economic system crashes. Liberians do not have financial problems only but trust problem.

The Fourth area: Huge administrative cost to run the government. The government of Liberia is involved with wasteful spending. It is impossible to govern the nation without God rightly. Considering this statement, let us hear what God has to say about why things are the way they are. Isaiah 56:11 (NAS) says, "And the dogs are greedy, they are not satisfied, and they are shepherds who have no understanding; They have all turned to their own way, each one to his unjust gain to the last one." Each government official turned to his dishonest gain from his quarter.

Dishonesty tends to be dominant among people of lower conscience. The New Revised Standard Bible says, "The dogs have mighty appetites, they are never full, they are the shepherds, but they don't understand—unable to comprehend the wants of the people spiritually all of them have turned to go their own ways, each one seeks his own gain." The New English Translation Bible says, "The dogs have big appetites; they are never full, they are shepherds who have no understanding; they all go their own way, each one looking for monetary gain." These different translations are used to underscore the emphasis on how our leaders ran the country. The government officials do not fear of God. They do not care about the people's welfare, but greed, power, and self; they only wanted to satisfy their own needs.

The financial crisis in a nation is always a failure on the part of the government. For many years, the government policy promotes reckless financial malpractices (moral hazards) through disruptive manipulations that have derailed the economy and caused a disastrous economic meltdown. It all begins when people entrusted with public funds begin to focus on themselves and spend less time thinking about the nation's future. Such opportunistic individuals only aligned themselves with their desires. The next government must scrutinize officials to restore accountability to keep this from happening again because the issue of character is such a central element of leadership—particularly about the kind of financial crisis we are in today. The past administration knew that all these behaviors and activities were the failure of character, yet she continued the path that sabotaged the economy. Value is an essential element that coexists with ethical or social dimensions such as honesty, integrity, compassion, fairness, charity, and social responsibility. When honesty meets with dishonesty, when fairness meets with pragmatism, or when national responsibility meets with personal interest, people become conflicted. Next, accuracy, dependability, and reliability are critical success factors in finance, but many of our leaders are error-prone dummies. Sometimes failure is the result of a lack of either management skills or trust—or a lack of both. Our government generates lots of money, but the profits never materialize to the extent necessary to sustain an ongoing economic growth. Government failure has created a misallocation and an inefficiency of resources in the nation. Government overspend worthlessly. I believe the government must dismiss and prosecute officials who artificially distort the efficient operation of the financial system.

The fifth area: Excessive bureaucracy has been one of the leading causes of government failure as well. Bureaucracy is a system of government in which most of the important decisions are made by state officials rather than by elected representatives. God has blessed us so abundantly with natural resources, so why are we experiencing so much unhappiness and discontentment? I believe the same God who has blessed us has provided the answer. Deuteronomy 8:18 (NAS) says, "But you shall remember the Lord your God, for it is He who is giving you power to make wealth, that He may confirm His covenant which He swore to your fathers, as it is this day." When the people in a nation turned their backs, and forget about the God who blessed them, they fail miserably. Liberia is a prime example. We have turned our backs on God; we lack the potential and wisdom to lead and transform the nation. There is a curse when we turn our backs on our creator. What then is the meaning of a curse? A curse is a release of spiritual and unseen forces that govern, direct, and guide the physical circumstances of a person or nation into negative and adverse circumstances. It is a spiritual weapon that binds and entangles the victim. The Aramaic word for curse is naqab - this is when a spiritual force carries out the following assignments: to stab, perforate, pierce, and strike through with violence. It also means "dries up," and it also refers to shrinkage by heat. A curse in a circumstance brings to the person or nation disgrace, confusion, shame, reproach, dishonor, and insignificance. It reduces the sufferer to a laughingstock before others. What Liberia is experiencing right now is because of selfish and ungodly leaders. The biggest problem with Liberia—bad leadership. Many of our leaders have been shaped by war, greed, corruption, and ignorance. God has given to us principles in the Bible so that we can approach national recovery with freedom, generosity, contentment, and confidence. We must act now because the failure to act is an action that is sure to fail.

King Solomon says in Proverbs 24:16, "The godly may trip seven times, but they will get up again, but one disaster is enough to overthrow the wicked." A man who says he does not make mistakes is not making progress, and the man who keeps making the same mistakes is not making progress either. If we do not follow God's instructions, we will have far greater problems than the financial failure we are experiencing now. Proverbs 13:18 says, "Poverty and shame will come to him who neglects discipline, but he who regards reproof will be honored." Matthew 22:29 (NLT) says, "Jesus replied, 'Your mistake is that you don't know the Scriptures, and you don't know the power of God.'" Tony Robbins, the noted author and motivation speaker said, "It's not what's happening to you now or what has happened in your past that determines who you become, rather it's your decisions about what to focus on, what things mean what to you, and what you're going to do about them that will determine your ultimate destiny." We must stop being so focused on self. Many people in this nation are consumed with the self. The "Me and I" generation is an old thing that has become the most influential element of our society. I believe this is one of the major areas of our financial failure. Many of the ills that plague our society are rooted in the self. We can name some here—theft, murder, immorality, greed, corruption, among others. These are rooted in self.

We are a nation that has become so obsessed with the self that we do not even care about others. We are running here and there, searching for answers to our financial failure, but God has provided the answers in Galatians 5:14. "You shall love your neighbor as yourself." Let's visit verse 15 together. It says, "But if you bite and devour one another, take care that you are not consumed by one another." I picked up an excerpt from an article that appeared in the Tallahassee Democrat on April 5, 1994. A woman commented on a child she had aborted by saying, "It wasn't a fetus. It was like cancer. It is okay to get this out of me, and let us get on with my life." You see, she only considered herself. Do you see what selfishness can cause? We are gathering facts about the root cause of our problems. The problem of self is neither new nor peculiar in our time. In this national recovery program, if we conquer the self, we have conquered all.

I hope we will all thoughtfully consider the words of Jesus in Matthew 16:24. "If anyone desires to come after me, let him deny himself, and take up his cross, and follow me." The older brother of the prodigal son in Luke 15 is an example of someone who had no compassion or love for others. He was self-centered. While the older brother seemed to love his father, his lack of love for his brother showed otherwise. Jesus stated to his disciples, "A new commandment I give to you, that you love one another; as I have loved you, that you also love one another" (John 13:34). We may claim to love God, but if, out of selfishness, we do not love our brother, we do not love God in reality. Karl Marx explains that the very idea of property makes people selfish and greedy. That is why wherever self-reigns supreme, there will be anarchy—a state of disorder due to the absence or nonrecognition of authority, a society of individuals who enjoy complete freedom to do what they want to do without law and order. Self-centeredness occurs when people are absorbed in themselves.

No one benefits from a selfish person. Philippians 2:3–4 says, "Do nothing from selfishness or empty conceit, but with humility of mind regard one another as more important than yourself; do not merely look out for your interest, but also for the benefit of others." James 3:16 says, "For where jealousy and selfish ambition exist, there is disorder and every evil thing." Do you see what is killing us? Social selfishness is one of the key areas that we need to look out for. Proverbs 11:26 says, "He who withholds grain, the people will curse him, but blessing will be on the head of the one who sells it." Jeremiah 45:5 says, "But you, are seeking great things for yourself, do not seek them; for behold, I am going to bring disaster on all flesh; declares the LORD, but I will give your life to you as booty in all the places where you may go." Selfishness has different forms, and it can disregard the rights of others. For this reason, mass unemployment and suffering is devastating the society. If the government can help reduce unemployment and mass suffering by making its citizens productive and resourceful, it can make a huge improvement in the economic welfare of the masses.

Through the lens of faith, this book will prepare us with knowledge and help us develop person so that we can have an excellent foundation, help the citizens gain a sense of fulfillment, commitment for the process and contentment in this recovery process. First Corinthians 10:33 says, "Just as I also please all men in all things, not seeking my own profit but the profit of the many so that they may be saved."

CHAPTER 7

How to Recover

Let us begin with the answer God has provided in this word for us on how to recover through his servant Job.

> Then Job answered the LORD and said, "I know that you can do all things; and that no purpose of yours can be thwarted. Who is this that hides counsel without knowledge? Therefore I have declared that which I did not understand, things too wonderful for me, which I did not know. Hear, now, and I will speak; I will ask you, and you instruct me. I have heard of you by the hearing of the ear: but now my eye sees you. Therefore I despise myself, and repent in dust and ashes." (Job 42:1–6)

We are still finding biblical answers to our national problems.

> Woe to those who decree iniquitous decrees, and the writers who keep writing oppression, to turn aside the needy from justice and to rob the poor of my people of their right, that widows may be their spoil, and that they may make the fatherless their prey! What will you do on the day of punishment, in the ruin that will come from afar? To whom will you flee for help, and where will you leave your wealth? Nothing remains but to crouch among the prisoners or fall among the slain. For all this, his anger

> has not turned away, and his hand is stretched out still. Woe to Assyria, the rod of my anger; the staff in their hands is my fury! (Isaiah 10:1–5)

Proverbs 3:5 says, "Trust in the LORD with all your heart and do not lean on your own understanding." The Lord restored the fortunes of Job when he prayed for his friends, and the Lord increased all that Job had twofold."(Job 42:10) What is God saying to us in this season of our national recovery? I believe it is God's predetermination for us to pray for one another and be reconciled as Job did. Let us consider the word reconciliation, the act of reconciling parties at variance, the renewal of friendship after a disagreement or enmity, the agreement of things seemingly opposite, different, or inconsistent.

Now before we go any further, we should look at the actual meaning of the function of the Truth and Reconciliation Commission (TRC), which was established in Liberia, according to Brian Rice and Anna Snyder.

> The role of Truth and Reconciliation Commission is to promote reconciliation within a society. There are five general aims of a TRC— (1) to discover, clarify, and formally acknowledge past abuses; (2) to respond to specific needs of victims; (3) to contribute to justice and accountability; (4) to outline institutional responsibility and recommend reforms; and (5) to promote reconciliation and reduce conflict." We can see clearly what is missing on the actual meaning and purpose of the TRC as it relates to Liberia. Therefore, things are the way they are today because the TRC in Liberia has not lived up to its purpose.

Let's take a closer look at the TRC by looking at Societal reconciliation. "Societal reconciliation is accomplished first by challenging the denial of atrocity. According to a Human Rights Watch report, "If a country is to come to terms with its past and successfully turn its attention to the future, it is essential that the truth of the past be officially established." It is impossible to expect "reconciliation" if part of the population refuses to accept that anything was ever wrong, and the other part has never received any acknowledgment of the suffering it has undergone or of the ultimate responsibility for that suffering."

"The primary goal of a TRC is to uncover the truth, reveal what happened, and prevent it from happening again. The truth about the past is very critical for societal reconciliation." For example, God said, "You shall not murder" (Exodus 20:13). Murder is the unlawful "killing of another person," but killing is a broader term. One can kill by accident or in self-defense, and it is not considered murder. This is why personal vengeance is considered lawlessness. Murder is killing, but killing is not necessarily murder. "Murder is a crime, which it constitutes unlawful homicide with malice aforethought or intentional and unlawful killing and is committed by somebody of sound mind and of the age of discretion with intent."

For true reconciliation to take place, capital punishment must be applied. Capital punishment is a capital offense; it is a crime that is treated so seriously that death may be considered a proper punishment. Let us be more specific about premeditated murder. Exodus 21:12–14 says, "He who strikes a man so that he dies shall surely be put to death, but if he did not lie in wait for him, but God let him fall into his hand, then I will appoint you a place to which he may flee. However, a man acts presumptuously toward his neighbor, so as to kill him craftily, you are to take him even from My altar, that he may die." Our Lord Jesus says in Matthew 5:17–18, "Think not that I am come to destroy the law or the prophets: I am not come to destroy, but to fulfill. For verily I say unto you, till heaven and earth pass, one jot or one little jot shall in no wise pass from the law, till all be fulfilled."

When confronting Governor Festus, Paul says in Acts 25:11, "If I am a wrongdoer, and have committed anything worthy of death, I do not refuse to die; but if none of these things is true of which these men accuse me, no one can hand me over to them. He both affirms capital statutes and accepts them as binding on him if he has broken one." The scriptures cannot be broken (John 10:35). This is why our society is broken down, and lawlessness is so rampant. The reason God established governments is to enforce laws. Let everyone be subject to the governing authorities, for there is no authority except that which God has established. The authorities that exist have been established by God. Consequently, whoever rebels against the authority is rebelling against what God has instituted, and those who do so will bring judgment on themselves. For rulers hold no terror for those who do right, but for those who do wrong. Do you want to be free from fear of the one in authority? Then do what is right and you will be commended. For the one in authority is God's servant for your good. But if you do wrong, be afraid, for rulers do not bear the sword for no reason. They are God's servants, agents of wrath to bring punishment on the wrongdoer."(Romans 13:1–4). Personally, I feel lots of anxiety about the future of our nation. I believe I am a realist and entirely pragmatic about the future of this country. Proverbs 16:9 says, "The mind of man plans his way, but the Lord directs his steps." I'll try to share as much as the Lord has led me to share about the past and present of our country. We will have to decide for ourselves if we want to do anything with this information.

This section of the book is written to heal broken relationships in our nation. As I am writing and also praying, this national recovery process will shape our individual lives, specifically how to act toward one another in our daily lives. We cannot say we are too busy dealing with current life in Liberia that we tend to forget history. My heart is to create awareness and to nurture interest for us to acknowledge the need for healing our wounds. I believe this will contribute to our national recovery. Even those in power now should break down the divided walls between the upper class and those who are increasingly marginalized and economically dominated in their own country. Those in leadership must recognize the greed and devastation that characterized their reason for coming to power and repent of their participation in the unjust exploitation of the masses.

We need to probe into the question of practical restitution and begin by trying to see the historical process through the eyes and the wounds of native Liberians. We who are descendants of ex-slaves called Americo-Liberian share a collective guilt for violating tribal ownership of land. We can start by probing questions of practical restitution, which is the restoration of something lost or stolen to its proper owner. And the system of restorative justice can be established. I believe this will enable us to revise the stance of triumphalist boasting and the celebration of supremacy for being called a Congo man or Congo woman. Our forefathers failed to realize they were benefitting from the exploitation of the natives and directly contributing to the destruction of other people's lives and communities just as the government does today.

The issue of restitution is God's idea shown in scriptures unraveling the heart and mind of God. In the Old Testament, the Israelites were under the law, which specified restitution in a variety of circumstances.

> If a man steals an ox or a sheep and slaughters it or sells it, he must pay back five head of cattle for the ox and four sheep for the sheep. A thief must certainly make restitution, but if he has nothing, he must be sold to pay for his" thief. If the stolen animal is found alive in his possession—whether ox or donkey or sheep—he must pay back double. If a man grazes his livestock in a field or vineyard and lets them stray and they graze in another man's field, he must make restitution from the best of his own field or vineyard. If a fire breaks out and spreads into thorn bushes so that it burns shocks of grain or standing grain or the whole field, the one who started the fire must make restitution. If a man borrows an animal from his neighbor and it is injured or dies … he must make restitution. (Exodus 22:1, 3–6, 14)

Leviticus 6:2–5 covers other situations in which the stolen property is restored plus one fifth of the value. Furthermore, the restitution was made to the owner of the property, not to the government or any other third party, and a guilt offering to the Lord would accompany the compensation. The Mosaic laws then protected victims of theft, extortion, fraud, and negligence by requiring the offending parties to make restitutions. The amount of remuneration varied anywhere from 100 to 500 percent of the loss. The restitution was made on the same day that the guilty one brought his sacrifice before the Lord, which implies that making amends with one's neighbor is just as important as making peace with God.

You may say, "But that's Old Testament. Let us wait and see." In the New Testament, we have the wonderful example of Zacchaeus in Luke 19. Jesus is visiting Zacchaeus's home, and the people who know the chief publican to be a wicked and oppressive man are beginning to murmur about his associating with a sinner. "But Zacchaeus stood up and said to the Lord, 'Lord here and Behold I give half of my possessions to the poor, and if I have cheated anybody out of anything, I will pay back four times the amount.' Jesus said to him, 'Today salvation has come to this house because this man too is a son of Abraham. For the Son of Man came to seek and to save what was lost'" (Luke 19:8–10).

From Zacchaeus's words, we gather that (1) he had been guilty of defrauding people, (2) he was remorseful over his past actions, and (3) he was committed to making restitution. From Jesus's words, we understand that (1) Zacchaeus was saved that day and his sin was forgiven and (2) the evidence of his salvation was both his public confession (Romans 10:10) and his relinquishing of all ill-gotten gains. Zacchaeus repented, and his sincerity was evident in his immediate desire to make restitution. Here was a man just like anyone of us. He was penitent and contrite, and the proof of his conversion to Christ was his resolve to atone as much as possible for past sin.

The same holds true for anyone who truly knows Christ today. Genuine repentance leads to a desire to redress wrong. When someone becomes a Christian, he or she will have a desire born of deep conviction to do things right, and that includes making restitution whenever possible. The idea of "whenever possible" is crucially important to remember. There are some crimes and sins for which there is no adequate restitution. In such instances, a Christian should make some form of restitution that demonstrates repentance. For instance, Zacchaeus, a tax collector who Jesus met, exemplified the beauty of restitution when confronted with his lifestyle of stealing under the guise of government work, which is similar to what many of our government officials are doing today, but Zacchaeus admitted his sin and restored to the people four times what he had stolen from them. Luke 19:7–10 says, "'He has gone to be the guest of a man who is a sinner,' Zacchaeus stopped and said to the Lord, 'Behold, Lord, half of my possessions I will give to the poor, and if I have defrauded anyone of anything, I will give back four times as much,' And Jesus said to him, 'today salvation has come to this house, because he too is a son of Abraham. For the Son of Man has come to seek and to save that which was lost.'"

In this process of our national recovery, God desires that we repent from our wickedness and follow him. Following him includes loving your neighbor. God is concerned about the heart first and foremost. Seeking to make restitution is evidence of a truly repentant heart. The true value is in the motivation leading to the action more than the action itself. A person sincerely seeking to make restitution is an individual who is willing to give up those things he once valued more the God's ways, seeking peace with his brother in love. Repentance without restitution is like faith without works. James 2:26 says, "For just as the body without the spirit is dead, so also faith without works is dead."

Before we go any further, we should distinguish economic growth from economic development, which many people use interchangeably. By economic growth, we mean the increase and quality of goods and services produced in the country, which in turn raises our national income. Like a human being, the economy cannot grow without maturing. Economic development talks about the maturity of the quality and quantity of goods and services produced in a country. This refers to the transformation of the country's income from primary to secondary sectors. The world degrades us when it refers to our economy as backward or underdeveloped.

On the other hand, when we talk about development, it means working with what we already have. When we reject development, we are bound to fail, and when we refuse to grow, we will always be stagnant. What we need to develop first is inside of us. The Bible says that a man's gift will make room for him. If we are not just satisfied with what other give us, that will certainly reduce the high level of dependency. One big reason we get so indebted is that we are classified as importers and not exporters. This always leads to a deficit balance of payment. Dependence on imports helps to stop our foreign exchange and renders us a debtor nation. Our economic situation is due to political instability.

So in our desire to recovery, we must realize that economic recovery cannot take place in a rowdy political atmosphere. Where there is a frequent change of governments, there are coups and counter-coups. No matter how much we desire success, economic recovery cannot be achieved in a disorderly society. This kind of atmosphere does not attract foreign or local investors to the country. I think one major factor that has led to economic failure is the lack of able leadership. I sang the song "Sweet Liberia" back in the days to let others know that we have a beautiful country of liberty where people from all occupations can find peace and a better life for their families. The type of leadership we had in the past contributed to where we find ourselves today.

I also believe that if we have able, honest, and dedicated leadership, we can achieve economic success in the shortest possible time. But if money earmarked for economic development is diverted into private purses or siphoned abroad for selfish motives, economic development will continue to be a ruse, and this dream will be far from reality. National recovery is very crucial at this time. The economic issue must be addressed with creative and responsible leadership that will take up the responsibility of establishing a godly system to secure the future and provide our people with hope for a better tomorrow. A key to defeating economic failure and poverty is to sacrifice immediate desires for long-term goals. This requires us to make right choices today for a better tomorrow.

Better leaders are produced only by the power of the Holy Spirit and the choices they make. The biblical solution we are searching for is not superficial or cheap but rather offers a real cure to the inner ethical cancer that is the root of our problem. We need to ask God for divine wisdom to instruct us. Psalm 32:8 says, "God promised David, 'I will instruct thee and teach thee in the way which thou shalt go, I will guide thee with mine eyes.'" Unfortunately, the past leaders of our country became increasingly ignorant of the means by which they could lead and bring change to the society, thus causing a growing feeling of apathy and economic despair.

A vital step to national recovery is through education. In fact, this is why this book is written. It helps us build opinions and make our points of view relevant to the circumstances surrounding us. For instance, Australia, the United States, and Japan are a few countries with very high literacy rates. These countries are extremely prosperous, and their citizens have a high income per capita. On the other hand, in underdeveloped and developing nations like ours, where the literacy rate is not as high, some people are still living below the poverty line. Education is vital for the economic prosperity of a nation. As we seriously read this book, it will save you from being fooled, cheated, or exploited. We live in a country where we are supposed to enjoy some rights and freedom, but it is easier to take advantage of innocent and illiterate people who are sometimes tricked into signing false documents or deprived of their rights. Unlike an educated person, they are not well aware of their rights and freedom.

An educated member of any society certainly has a greater chance to contribute to his or her community. Education helps you become an active member of the society and participate in the ongoing changes and developments once we become knowledgeable on the issues and act upon that knowledge. Education helps you become a useful member of the society. But here is the thing. We do not just need literate people in government. We need educated ones too. Liberia is at a crossroad. We do not just want government officials who can read and write but produce no results. As a researcher, I also discovered that information and education bring out the best in an ugly situation but never resolve to the use of propaganda. The difference between these two methods is that education will lead people into a proper understanding of the truth, while propaganda wants people to accept a viewpoint without proper consideration of the facts.

CHAPTER 8

Keys to National Recovery

Keys to National Recovery

The word key speaks of authority. Authority is power delegated to our leaders to cast the vision of national recovery that will be the power invested in the citizens by the government we serve. Key speaks of access—the right to use something. The people need to have access to education, high-skilled jobs, empowerment, and the vast natural resources. And key also speaks of control—control over what we have to manage properly, effectively, and efficiently.

What does the term economic recovery mean? "An economic recovery occurs when an economy strengthens after a period of recession." Liberia is one of least developed, least stable economic countries in West Africa. The country has been suffering from long-term political strife and a severely depressed economy. From Quizlet.com we can state that an economic recovery is the phase of the "business cycle following a recession during which an economy regains and exceeds peak employment and output levels achieved before the downturn." A recession is a significant decline in activities across the economy because of poor management by those in power. As a developing nation, we have suffered major setbacks, and I think this is due to failed government policies that we must not repeat if we want to prevent a similar financial crisis and economic meltdown.

Often when there is a national situation in the country concerning moral, political, or economic challenges, it is important that we come up with a solution via the Word of God. Second Chronicles 7:14 says, "If my people who are called by my name humble themselves, and pray and seek my face and turn from their wicked ways, then I will hear from heaven and will forgive their sin and heal their land." If there is no repentance, there will be no healing or recovery. God promised to do three things: he will hear from heaven, forgive our sins, and heal our land, while we are to do four things: to humble, to pray, to seek the face of God, and turn away from our wicked ways. The first thing to remember is that God is referring to the nation of Israel. Verse 14 starts right in the middle of a sentence. It is not a complete thought on its own. The preceding verse speaks about how God will withhold rain, send locusts, or allow pestilence to come upon the nation Israel. "My people, who are called by my name." Who are these people? These people are not Liberians; actually, they are Israelites. But if we obey God's commands and turn from our wicked ways, he will also restore and bless our land. the nation of Israel had a unique arrangement with God if they obeyed his commandments, God would bless the land and allow them to stay on it. We have to understand that recovery or restoration of our land is in obedience to God's commandments. We have to repent and ask God for forgivingness. Psalm 80:3 says, "O God, restore us and cause your face to shine upon us, and we will be saved." It is clearly seen that biblical pathway is key to our economic recovery process. The national recovery process is not something one man can do alone; it must be done collectively. Henceforward, we all have to come to the place of recoverability. In Genesis 1:28, God granted dominion to the humankind under his law, but he did not grant his sovereignty to them. One of the keys to national recovery is realizing that in an ultimate sense, just like with Israel, all property belongs to the Lord. As Leviticus 25:23 (NIV) made clear, "The land is mine and you are but aliens and my tenants." If we understand that everything belongs to God, we will know how to treat one another so that we do not fail in this process. The poor leadership in the past focused more on nepotism and kleptocracy than creating national unity to develop the country. Those members of the previous leadership became a classic example of the oppressed becoming the oppressors. Let's take a look at these two words to gain a deeper understanding. Nepotism is the unfair use of power to get jobs or other benefits for your family or friends. It is patronage bestowed or favoritism shown by family relationship as in business and politics. A kleptocracy is a government or state in which those in power exploit national resources and steal, and this had been the trend of every government in this nation ... till now.

First John 3:17 says, "But whoever has this world's goods, and sees his brother in need, and shuts up his heart from him, how does the love of God abide in him?" All of us possess goods in one way or another - "this includes either possessions or property. We could translate goods as "means of living. Anyone who has any resources for the maintenance of life has something to give to others. Giving to others does not require wealth; "but one can make financial sacrifices for the advancement of others. Leaders with true vision seek the well-being of all those who are affected by the economy. One major key is that the Bible is particular about defending the rights of the alien, the poor, or the disadvantaged. "Administer true justice, do not oppress the widow, the orphan, the alien or the poor; and do not devise evil in your hearts against one another" (Zechariah 7:10). "Do not take advantage of a hired man who is poor and needy, whether he is one of your countrymen or one of your aliens who is in your land in your towns" (Deuteronomy 24:14).

There is an article titled "Liberia's Ugly Past" by James Smith extensively states, "Unfortunately, those who came here as freed slaves brought with them some of the attributes of America, a society which had consigned them to subhuman conditions, considered them as property for nearly two and quarter centuries before they emigrated to Liberia. Instead of being guided against such inhumane treatment, they suffered at the hands of their former masters. They took on the characters of the slave masters and began to treat the natives similarly to what they had experienced in slavery." The freed-slaves' "rationale was that the natives were hostile elements opposed to the ex-slaves who had come to take their land. No doubt they engaged the settlers in a battle for control of their land, which was taken from them through all kinds of fraudulent schemes.

The unfortunate saga of Liberian history (which most Liberians do not know about) is that the struggle for equality, equity, justice, and fair treatment for all Liberians is as old as the republic." Many had the false impression that Liberia was a "microcosm of the United States in Africa, that we had a similar government structure—legislative, executive, and judicial branches. But the truth is that all legislation was drafted—not only proposed—from the executive mansion and then sent to the so-called legislators, who merely rubber-stamped the laws." The outcomes of all cases involving the government were essentially determined by the president. In other words, the Liberian president was an absolute ruler. It is almost the same today as it was "during the heyday of the True Whig Party rule. It was difficult to distinguish between official and private business."

Key legislators were agents of foreign corporations, making laws against the citizens' interests to benefit the foreign companies they represented. Most government officials, including the president, vice president, and the speaker of the house of representatives, where shareholders and board members of corporations that had joint venture agreements with foreign businesses. The concept of conflict of interest (i.e., the possibility of a clash between self-interest and public interest) had no meaning in Liberia's officialdom." Is there any difference today? Just as it was in the days of the True Whig Party, so it has been till now.

Today "the government sides with foreign corporations by making laws that depress the wages of the peasant workers while top officials receive kickbacks from these same corporations. Corruption is the mother's milk of Liberian politics." There are also poor political and economic conditions that permeated the Liberian society just like before. Unfortunately, my brothers and sisters whose ancestors were brought here to Liberia (formerly called Costa da Pimenta, which means Pepper Coast or Grain Coast) as freed slaves hundreds of years ago continued to treat the natives as economic aliens and refused to integrate them into the economic mainstream." Today they are still treating the native people differently across borders, making them feel like alien outcasts, but a true leader who means well should try to allocate resources fairly and pay equal attention to all.

The situation is a problem within a problem." The vision of a just leader should echo the last words of King David: "When one rules over men in righteousness—he is like the light of morning at sunrise on a cloudless morning, like the brightness after rain that brings grass from the earth" (2 Samuel 23:4). A just and fair leader will ensure that his or her people have enough productive capacity and consumable resources to survive the crisis and prosper. My antidote is to this problem is to officially encourage whistleblowers to expose injustices and errors so we, the nation can act promptly. A government must live by its values. It is difficult to keep people motivated and loyal if they feel those at the top are taking advantage of them.

To recover, we must deal with the problem effectively. We must know the cause or causes. James D. Smith further states the basic premise. "The Americo-Liberians are the only people who can rule Liberia ... Native people are incapable of ruling Liberia." Many Americo-Liberians still believe that they must rule the country, or else Liberia should not exist." For people like us who are interested in something more than a second-grade understanding of Liberian history want to go deeper because this threatens the nation's economic survival. "There is no distinction between Jew and Gentile, for the same Lord is Lord over all [of us], and [He is] abounding in riches (blessing) for all who call on him [in faith and prayer]." God is showing us that there should be no difference between the Americo-Liberians and the natives Liberians. I believe this is the root cause of our problem, and God's heart beat to us is no segregation. Let's hear from God's perspective. First Timothy 6:5_9 (NAS) says,

> And constant friction between men of depraved mind and deprived of the truth, who suppose that godliness is a means of gain, but godliness is a means of great gain when accompanied by contentment. For we brought nothing into the world, so we cannot take anything out of it either, if we have food and covering, with these we shall be content, but those who want to get rich fall into temptation and a snare and many foolish and harmful desire which plunge men into ruin and destruction.

Let us look at another key. "David reigned over all Israel, doing what was just and right for all his people" (2 Samuel 8:15). Each of us in this economic recovery and the transformational process has the capacity to lead not only as a source of economic gain but also as a force for economic and social justice. Leaders who want to succeed in this recovery program must be credible and must value fairness to all Liberians and act in consonance with those values even when it is uncomfortable or difficult. The new generation of leaders must be concerned for the economically and socially disadvantaged—not just for their gain but the nation's profitability. I believe this is the pathway to national recovery.

CHAPTER 9

The Quest for Transformation

We, humans are spiritual beings in physical bodies with minds (souls) to do what the Holy Spirit teaches. A quest is defined as a long search for something that is difficult to find; it is about seeking something important. This study is about the desire for transformation, and it often involves a journey.

The issue of spiritual transformation is not new in the Christian faith. It has been a primary issue for many years, though perhaps given different labels throughout church history. From the time the Spirit of God descended upon the believers in Jerusalem, God has been transforming the souls of individuals in the context of universal and local Christian communities. (Bible.org, n.d.)

The word transformed in Romans 12:2 is a Greek word metamorphosis. (Meta means change, and morph means form.) The word essentially refers to a change in form. In common practice, the word transformation is used to describe the change of a rather unattractive chrysalis (larva) into a beautiful butterfly. Christ's transfiguration in Mark 9:2–13 was a metamorphosis. The Lord wants each of us to be transformed, and this is accomplished by having a renewed mind. Our mind must be changed in such a way that the old nature with its values, beliefs, and practices is replaced by that which conforms to the mind of Christ. We are not genetically programmed to transform ourselves. God will not do it for us automatically. Nor will he force it upon us. He will only do it as we allow him and cooperate with Him in the process - walk in the Spirit. (Shober, n.d.)

Life is real when it is transformed. Research shows that

> Monarch butterflies follow a very specific generational migration that starts in Mexico. During the first generation, they will fly to the southern United States, where they will remain for life. Their offspring will fly to the central states, stopping somewhere around the Ohio River, where they will reproduce. At this point, the third generation will migrate to Canada to lay eggs. The fourth generation that is born in Canada will then take a miraculous flight all the way back to the same mountains in Mexico where their great-grandparents originated. For countless years this incredible butterfly has been following this same four-generation cycle, which seems incredible and mysterious in the natural world. In short, they do it because it is in their nature. Paul said in Romans 12:2, "Be transformed by the renewing of your mind." The word Paul uses here is the word we use to describe the metamorphosis of a butterfly. The change, in the end, makes for something completely different than what was there before. This is how total the transformation should be when it comes to our thinking. And remember, our thoughts determine our actions. (Crenshaw, 2010).

For Liberia to be transformed and experience greatness, there must be a spiritual quest for transformation, and it all starts in our hearts. God is speaking to the nation through this scripture. Jeremiah 24:7 says, "I will give them a heart to know Me, for I am the LORD; and they will be my people, and I will be their God, for they will return to Me with their whole heart." Now he speaks to us as individuals. Ezekiel 36:26 says, "Moreover, I will give you a new heart and put a new spirit within you; and I will remove the heart of stone from your flesh and give you a heart of flesh." This is the corporate dimension of spiritual transformation. Ezekiel 11:19 says, "And I will give them one heart, and put a new spirit within them, and I will take the heart of stone out of their flesh and give them a heart of flesh." We have to be willing to go through a process of change similar to that of a butterfly. Warner further explains

It behooves us to understand the metamorphosis of the butterfly and think about how the spiritual parables match with our lives. The butterfly begins as a small egg. It grows into a little caterpillar that does nothing but eats and grows bigger and bigger and bigger. Then it spins a cocoon away from the view of the world and slowly is transformed. Suddenly, it emerges with wings. The life cycle of the butterfly is a metamorphosis. All butterflies go through four separate stages in their life cycle—the egg, caterpillar, pupa (chrysalis), and the butterfly.

My prayer is the Lord give us the greater understanding of how he wants us to be transformed through this national recovery process. Let's compare this physical process to how we're being prepared for greatness.

The Greek word metamorphosis is used four times in the New Testament. Matthew 17:2 (KJV) says, "And was transfigured before them; and his face did shine as the sun, and his raiment was white as the light." Mark 9:2 (NAS) says, "Six days later, Jesus took with him Peter and James and John, and brought them up on a high mountain by themselves; and he was transfigured before them." Romans 12:2 (KJV) says, "And be not conformed to this world; but be ye transformed by the renewing of your mind, that ye may prove what is that good, and acceptable, and perfect, will of God." II Corinthians 3:18 (KJV) says, "But we all with open face beholding as in a glass the glory of the Lord, are changed into the same image from glory to glory, even as by the Spirit of the Lord. (Warner, n.d.).

"Dr. Robert B. Cialdini recounts a study that was done at a horse track. The two psychologists who led the study found that people were much more confident in the horse they chose immediately after they placed a bet when just seconds before they had randomly selected the horse. Once they made a public declaration by laying money down on a particular horse, they matched their feelings to their actions. (Crenshaw, 2010)

This is how a transformed life is supposed to feel. We match everything we do with our new lives. It is very hard for people to change their opinions, let alone change the opinion of another person. We've all seen people become trapped by their words instead of confessing to a fault. They will defend their words and actions all to appear right or at least avoid appearing weak.

Paul says that our thoughts become brand new in Christ. In Christ, we are not trying to defend the self. We are surrendering to him and going through a complete metamorphosis apart from other people's opinions. When our thinking is changed, our beliefs are changed. Our actions are changed, and our life is changed.

> In the 1970s, a woman named Laura Shultz, who was sixty-three at the time, lifted the back end of a buck off of her grandson's arm. Peak performance author Dr. Charles Garfield tried to get an interview with her, but she refused, unwilling to talk about the event. After much convincing, she finally told him she did not like to think about what happened. "If I was able to do this when I didn't think I could, what does that say about the rest of my life? Have I wasted it?" Charlie could coach her so that she could pursue her dreams. At sixty-three, she went back to school, got a degree in geology, and became a professor at a local college. That happened when she changed her beliefs. Her thoughts about what was and was not possible were transformed. As Lily Tomlin said, "I always wanted to be somebody, but I should have been more specific." You can make a difference today. Even if you have to admit you were wrong, make a phone call, give an apology, and be transformed by renewing your mind. (Crenshaw, 2010)

To understand our need for transformation, we must understand who we are currently, both as individuals and as members of the body of Christ. Who our past has undoubtedly shaped us. Therefore, we explore various aspects of our identities, including our heritage and temperament. What do these tell us about who we are and what we value? It can take a long time—sometimes more than a lifetime—for the Spirit of God to transform our values so that we align with our new identities in Christ. We cooperate with the Spirit when we reflect on what our values are and how well they line up with our identities in Christ as described in scripture. One of the most significant characteristics of our identity in Christ is that we are now part of the body of Christ. The Christian life cannot be lived in isolation (Your Identity and community, n.d.) when we are transformed.

Involvement in other people's lives requires more than what the term fellowship has too often come to mean. Real involvement includes holding certain values in common and practicing a lifestyle we believe is noble while appreciating that this lifestyle does not make us perfect. This lifestyle is a commitment to let God continue to form us spiritually. (Main and Oklahoma Church of Christ, McAlester, Oklahoma, 2010) A caterpillar changing into a butterfly is an excellent picture of what the Bible speaks of concerning the transformation of the believers into the image of Christ.

The word transformation, according to Merriam-Webster's, means "a complete or major change in someone or something's appearance, form." This gives us a basic definition of transformation as a kind of change. Again, in the original Greek language of the New Testament, the word for transformation is metamorphosis. The same biological definition for metamorphosis, also according to Merriam-Webster's, is "a profound change in form from one stage to the next in the life history of an organism as from a caterpillar to a pupa and from the pupa to the adult butterfly." Although an outward change in appearance or form takes place, the change comes from within the life of the organism. A caterpillar is born with the life that causes it to become a butterfly. It does not put on a butterfly costume or strive to act like a butterfly. As long as it eats, its metabolism takes the nutrients it consumes, assimilates them into the caterpillar, and causes it to grow so that eventually, the caterpillar changes and becomes a genuine butterfly (Bibles for America Podcast, 2016)

> "When we pray to receive Christ as our Savior, we are regenerated or reborn with God's life to become children of God. We are reborn with the divine life of God within. This life transforms us into the image of Christ." (Bibles for America Podcast, 2016) But there must be a quest for transformation for that to happen. "Like the caterpillar, we must stay in the process of transformation by eating the bread of life. In John 6:35, Jesus said, "I am the bread of life; he who comes to me shall by no means hunger,

and he who believes in me shall by no means ever thirst."
Bibles for America Podcast, 2016)

My dear reader, transformation is not a change brought about by you simply doing good or improving your behavior. Imagine a man who is undernourished, sickly, and pale. Now imagine you put makeup on him to improve his appearance. He may look healthier, but the makeup is only cosmetic, something externally applied. What he needs is a genuine change from within. This is what is happening to a lot of people in this country; their life is cosmetic. Now if that same undernourished, pale man were to start eating healthy, nourishing food, a noticeable change would begin to occur. His color would improve, and his body would be strengthened. Eventually, his appearance would become healthy not because of something they did outwardly but because of something that changed inwardly.

As we end this topic, we want to go back to the foundation to understand the quest for transformation and how we need to understand the definitions of transformation. As the KJV Dictionary defines transform: "1 To change the form of; to change the shape or appearance; to metamorphose; as a caterpillar transformed into a butterfly. 2 in theology, to change the natural disposition and temper of man from a state of enmity to God and his law, into the image of God, or into a disposition and temper conformed to the will of God. Be ye transformed by the renewing of your mind." To have a fruitful and productive transformation process, Liberians have to be transformed to change the nation because what is on the inside of us will reflect in our nation.

CHAPTER 10

National Transformation

Indeed, this is a great honor, and I am very pleased to share some biblical thoughts with you. No individual alone can lead this nation out of our current situation. We need to start embracing biblical paradigms and principles that will lead to greater unity and impact for the whole nation. Bear in mind that our Lord's patience is meant to lead us to salvation. As it is stated in 2 Peter 3:10-18

So then, dear friends, since you are looking forward to this, make every effort to be found spotless, blameless and at peace with him. 15 Bear in mind that our Lord's patience means salvation, just as our dear brother Paul also wrote you with the wisdom that God gave him. He writes the same way in all his letters, speaking in them of these matters. His letters contain some things that are hard to understand, which ignorant and unstable people distort, as they do the other Scriptures, to their own destruction. Therefore, dear friends, since you have been forewarned, be on your guard so that you may not be carried away by the error of the lawless and fall from your secure position. But grow in the grace and knowledge of our Lord and Savior Jesus Christ. To him be glory both now and forever! Amen.

The error of twisting the truth in this nation is lawlessness. Does our understanding of transformation lead to lawfulness or lawlessness? "In fact, what is the error of lawlessness? Everyone who practices sin also practices lawlessness, and sin is lawlessness (1 John 3:4)." (Broer, 2013) This scripture informs us that we have been characterized by lawlessness as a nation, and this is why we need a paradigm shift. I pray that this will be a challenge to us about transformation.

"A paradigm is a framework for understanding the way the world operates around us." A paradigm shift takes place when we are led to believe, think, and act in a new way" (Pagh, 2014) that does not conform to the systems of the world. That is why we are instructed by God not to conform to the way of the world. There are some biblical recommendations in this book that represent an important paradigm shift and that our leaders must embrace and implement for sustained transformation to take place. We see that in the mandate Pagh asserts "the Great Commission. It is not just about individuals." It also talks about the discipleship of nations. Matthew 28:18–20 says, And Jesus came up and spoke to them, saying, 'All authority has been given to me in heaven and on earth. Go therefore and make disciple of all the nations, baptizing them in the name of the Father and the Son and the Holy Spirit, teaching them to observe all that I commanded you; and lo, I am with you always, even to the end of the age. This means we can be shaped by the life of Christ in such a way that, in conforming to biblical values, it will manifest a change in behavior.

In the Bible, transformation means "change or renewal from a life that no longer conforms to the ways of the world to one that pleases God." This is accomplished by the renewing of our minds—an inward spiritual transformation that will manifest itself in outward actions. The concept of transformational leadership in a nation is multifaceted, but "the power of transformation comes from only one source. Paul said, "For the message of the cross [the gospel] is foolishness to those who are perishing, but to us who are being saved it is the power of God" (1 Corinthians 1:18)." (gotquestions.org) Liberia needs national transformation if we desire to recover, and it is only through the gospel message of Christ that we learn "to put off our old self, which belongs to our former manner of life that is corrupt through deceitful desires, and to put on the new self, created after the likeness of God in true righteousness and holiness" (Ephesians 4:22–24). "For if you live according to the sinful nature, you will die; but if by the Spirit you put to death the misdeeds of the body, you will live, because those who are led by the Spirit of God are the sons of God"

(Romans 8:13–14). (gotquestions.org)

The Bible presents the transformed life in Christ as demonstrated through our "bearing fruit in every good work and growing in the knowledge of God" (Colossians 1:10). (gotquestions.org) Those who were once far from God are transformed then they are "drawn near" to him through the blood of Christ (Ephesians 2:13) (gotquestions.org). Romans 12:2 says, "And do not be conformed to this world, but be transformed by the renewing of your mind, so that you may prove what the will of God is, that which is good and acceptable and perfect." (gotquestions.org) First, I want to establish the fact that transformation is a thing of the mind. "As a man thinks in his heart or mind so is he" (Proverbs 23:7). This principle must be fulfilled as a cardinal requirement to build up our capacity to congregate the citizens and invoke obedience in harvesting national transformation.

Leadership that enables national transformation must be a leader who has been impacted in such a way that he or she has become a disciple of Jesus. It is this kind of quality leadership that gives rise to national transformation so that the people of the nation can reflect the character of Christ. Liberia needs transformational leaders to serve as key mobilizers for national development. If this quality is properly harvested, it will lead Liberia to greatness.

It is important to stress that the effective exercise of leadership comes from setting up a vision, developing an agenda, and mobilizing the citizens. Leaders can then provide definition and direction that can serve as a rallying point for many to follow. Former president Eisenhower of the United States once defined leadership as the "ability to decide what is to be done and then to get others to want to do it." Harry Truman put it more pungently when he said, "A leader is a man who has the ability to get other people to do what they don't want to do and like it." These two leaders of the United States of America perceived leadership in terms of a man's ability to manage men in such a way as to get certain results willingly. Therefore, it is imperative that the transformed leadership incorporate these key biblical paradigms and principles into their vision and the mission to achieve national transformation. During the middle of the Second World War, C. S. Lewis wrote a short essay for the Spectator on "Equality." In it, he said, "Mankind is so fallen that no man can be trusted with unchecked power over his fellows." There is a cry for biblical understanding about humanity and personhood in these critical periods when the cry for true freedom, dignity, and transformation is desperately needed. We need to get from where we are to become a nation where all people can learn the way they were designed to be and act.

We truly need to transform rather than reform.

The government needs to transform the educational system because knowledge is power after all. Hosea 4:6 says, "My people are destroyed for lack of knowledge. Because you have rejected knowledge, I also will reject you from being my priest. You have forgotten the law of your God, and I also will forget your children." The necessary transformation should most likely be led first by parents, concerned citizens, and the government. The need for transformation is more apparent today in Liberia than ever before. The world around us is changing rapidly in ways that have powerful implications for transformation. All through biblical history, the role that the scriptures played in the transformation of a nation is highly illuminating with tremendously useful and insightful lessons. In this time of national transformation, our leaders must focus on the Liberian people instead of themselves. The merger of self and the citizens are always rocky and can lead to the downfall of the leaders.

"Moses was a leader who inherited a lot of problems, but the strength of his vision and his commitment to Israel's mission made him the ultimate visionary. People would follow him through even the most adverse circumstances." (Woolfe, 2002) This book is meant to encourage and strengthen those who will lead the new Liberia, assisted by divine intervention. It will take a great and inspiring leader to initiate national transformation and replace those government officials who are depleting our resources. I'm sorry to say, most of our past leaders possessed vast academic knowledge from some of the best schools in the world but lacked results. Samson, for example, had physical strength, but he had some tremendous weaknesses and blind spots in his interpersonal judgment and leadership style. The emphasis in this book on national recovery is meant to provide inspiration and purpose. Long speeches and oaths are not necessary to impress people with one's integrity. Matthews 5:33-37 says "Again, you have heard that it was said to those of ancient times, 'You shall not swear falsely, but carry out the vows you have made to the Lord.' But I say to you, Do not swear at all, either by heaven, for it is the throne of God, or by the earth, for it is his footstool, or by Jerusalem, for it is the city of the great King. And do not swear by your head, for you cannot make one hair white or black. Let your word be 'Yes, Yes' or 'No, No'; anything more than this comes from the evil one." In the wake of the political upheaval, politicians are contending, and people are swayed this way and that way by conflicting tides of interest and a passion for the power behind the throne. In the face of obfuscations like these, our yes should be yes, and our no be no. The case study we are about to do depicts the situation we are in. So let's go back a few thousand years to Nehemiah, whose integrity inspired the people of Judah to rebuild the temple in fifty-two days. Nehemiah 6:15 says, "So the wall was completed on the twenty-fifth of the month Elul, in fifty-two days." From this account, you will see that it is not that difficult to build Liberia and achieve national transformation despite the obstacles. But people who lack integrity usually show it in a variety of ways. Nehemiah was appointed governor by King Artaxerxes, and he could have enriched himself and used any means at his disposal to complete the temple.

"Moreover, from the day that I was appointed to be their governor in the land of Judah, from the twentieth year to the thirty-second year of King Artaxerxes, for twelve years, Neither I nor my brothers ate the food allotted to the governor, But the earlier governors ... placed a heavy burden on the people and took forty shekels of silver from them in addition to food and wine, But ... I did not act like that, Instead, I devoted myself to the work on this wall ... we did not acquire any land ... furthermore, a hundred and fifty Jews and officials ate at my table ... Each day one ox, six choice sheep, and some poultry were prepared for me ... in spite of all this, I never demanded the food allotted to the governor, because the demanded were heavy on these people". (Nehemiah 5:14–18) "Note that Nehemiah refused to appropriate more than he was entitled to. He did not ask for the full amount of what he was entitled to, but rather he shared what he had with his followers. He did this for the sake of the people and for rapid completion of the task."

There can be no excuse for the underdevelopment of Liberia as it is today. The prophets were the people who kept the nation of Israel honest just like us today. "When the people lost sight of the commandments dealing with honesty and integrity, again, prophets arose to remind them where true north lay on the compass when the whole nation was taking a moral turn to the south."(Woolfe, 2002) Does it look like Liberia today? There are people in Liberia who claimed to be prophets, giving direction to the nation, and they often mislead many. Ezekiel prophesied against false prophets, those with "false words, lying visions … and utter lying divinations." Ezekiel 13:8–9 says, "Today we speak of those who varnish or whitewash the truth by putting a pleasing patina on top of a weak or faulty structure (Woolfe)." Again, several thousand years ago, Ezekiel addressed this universal problem by using a very similar analogy to ours. When a flimsy wall is built, they cover it with "whitewash." "Therefore, tell those who cover it with whitewash that it is going to fall … when it falls, you will be destroyed in it … So I will spend my wrath against the wall and against those who covered it with whitewash, I will say to you, 'The wall is gone, and so are those who whitewash it'" (Ezekiel 13:10–16). This is what happens to a nation when the people's activities are based on falsehood. In Ezekiel's proclamations, he is saying that there can be no true peace and harmony in a nation either in business or politics without true honesty and integrity. My friends, listen to me. Whitewashing may seem to work in the short run, but it doesn't in the long run.

I believe we are being transformed by these biblical truths. During the time of the prophet Jeremiah, the people were very corrupt like us today. Liberia is even more corrupt now than it was in the late eighteenth and nineteenth centuries and will continue to be corrupt if no radical actions are taken. Jeremiah continuously "spoke out about the lack of integrity that permeated the entire society, which did not make him a revered guest of honor at the king's court or banquets."(woolfe) Today many of our so-called bishops are silent on national issues, but a prophet who points out the leader's lack of integrity is not necessarily going to be popular in society. "Go up and down the streets of Jerusalem (Liberia), look around, and search through the square. If you can find one person who deals honestly and seeks the truth, I will forgive this city (Monrovia). Even though they say, "Assuredly as the Lord lives," still they are swearing falsely" (Jeremiah 5:1–2). The prophet Isaiah also lived in an era like ours. "Honesty and integrity were not the foundations of the nation of Israel. He saw a vision of the Lord surrounded by angels." (Woolfe, 2002) He looked down at himself and realized just how morally far he and his nation had sunk. Our leaders need to see this in themselves. He said, "'Woe to me,' I cried, 'I am ruined I am man of unclean lips, and I live among a people of unclean lips.'" Isaiah was probably the "cleanest-lipped" guy in town, but he identified with the problem. (Woolfe, 2002)

I have come to realize that in a corrupt society, all can possibly get corrupted. The ethical standards of a nation are judged by its actions, not by pious statements of intent. "Whether in the short run or in the long run, dishonesty has a way of being exposed." (Woolfe, 2002) So, to recover nationally and experience transformation, we must be people of integrity and honesty. Individuals tend to exercise increased integrity and honesty when the culture supports these behaviors. In these times, strong individuals must maintain these traits, particularly when they are in opposition to the powers that be, who have no checks, balances, or rules. The rule of law is repeated many times in the Bible as actual laws to govern a nation. There are particularly strong warnings about the abuses of power by those in "authority as well as commands for leaders and followers at all levels to behave ethically. The following passages were written by Moses centuries before Saul came to power and were anointed the first king of Israel. Moses was keenly aware of the potential abuse of authority by any leader (Woolfe, 2002). Many of our government officials are abusing their power today, no matter how upright they pretend to be. Therefore, Moses suggested some safeguards, which we have too often ignored in selecting our modern political leaders. "The King ... must not acquire great numbers of horses for himself or make the people return to Egypt to get more of them ... He must not take too many wives, or his heart will be led astray, He must not accumulate large amounts of silver and gold, when he takes the throne of his kingdom, he is to write for himself on a scroll a copy of this law ... He should not consider himself better than his brothers and turn from the law to the right or left" (Deuteronomy 17:14–20). Some people never learn their lesson in life. One of the most dishonest men in the Bible was Judas Iscariot, one of Jesus's disciples who betrayed him mostly out of greed. The story of Zacchaeus shows us that people who have lost their integrity can find it. Zacchaeus was a tax collector for the Roman government. Like many of our government officials today, being a tax collector was one the least popular professions in ancient Israel, but he was not beyond rehabilitation. Because he was a short man, he climbed a tree so he could clearly see and hear this mysterious prophet Jesus. Jesus's response was to invite himself to the home of this social outcast. There is hope for you. "'Zacchaeus, come down immediately, for I must stay at your house today' … All the people saw this and began to mutter, 'He has gone be the guest of a sinner.' But Zacchaeus stood up and said … 'look Lord Here and now I give half of my possessions to the poor, and if I have cheated anybody out of anything, I will pay him back four times the amount'" (Luke 19:1–8).

The interesting thing about this country is that almost everyone says he or she is honest but doesn't think that others are actually honest. This is the reality of where we are today as a nation. Everyone is always looking over the shoulder of his or her neighbor, pointing fingers at others as well as the government for our problems. Everyone else wants to blame others and keeps them accountable, forgetting that the real measure of honesty and accountability begins with ourselves. And that's exactly what Zacchaeus did, dealing with personal issues in his life. Indeed, the life of Zacchaeus serves as a daily reminder of how honesty, integrity, and accountability can be used as tools to address the current state of the country and help us achieve the objectives of national transformation.

According to the Advanced Learner's Dictionary, national is defined as "connected with a particular nation, shared by a whole nation." Development is defined as "the gradual growth of something so that it becomes more advanced or stronger." Our country is a total mess. There are many voices saying Liberia will rise again which sounds good, but I think that is an understatement, without proper actions. "Actions speak louder than words."(Anonymous, n.d.) "We are all familiar with what happened to Pharaoh and his men when they tried to pursue the Israelites across the dry bed of the Red Sea, which had been parted for the fugitives. Seas may part for people of honor and integrity, but they often rush back to drown those whose words mean nothing to themselves or others." Too often, it seems honesty, integrity, and accountability do not pay off in the short term, whereas dishonesty and a lack of integrity do. How often have we heard sayings like "Do unto others before they can do unto you" or "No good deed will go unpunished?" In the Bible as in a nation, wrongdoers ultimately receive their proper consequences, and virtuous people earn their just rewards.

"One test of a leader's integrity is his or her attitude toward public property." Liberia is bleeding because of this. Some of our leaders want everything for themselves, while others refuse to take a penny of funds with which they have been entrusted. What kind of leader are you? In recent times, I read of leaders like Ferdinand Marcos and his wife, Imelda. (She owns a thousand of pairs of shoes.) And they appropriated much of their country's wealth before they absconded to a foreign country. Let us compare our national leaders, who are leaving state power, to that of Samuel, who presided as high priest of Israel for several decades. As you will notice, not only did he refuse to take anything not belonging to him, but he also asked his countrymen to identify anything that he had accumulated through the power of his office. Then he would quickly and cheerfully return it.

"Here I stand, Testify against me in the presence of the Lord. … Whose ox have I taken? Whose donkey have I taken? Whom have I cheated? Whom have I oppressed? From whose hand have I taken a bribe to make me shut my eyes? If I have done any of these, I will make it right." "You have not cheated or oppressed us," they replied, "You have not taken anything from anyone's hand." (1 Samuel 12:1–4)

How many of our government officials and political leaders would willingly open themselves up to such scrutiny? Samuel did not passively respond or react to an investigation of his possessions like many of us are doing today, even the so-called Christians? He initiated it himself. He invited the investigation of his honesty and integrity down to the last ox and donkey, promising to return anything that might have been immorally appropriated. No matter how insignificant, he promised to rectify the least evidence of impropriety or dishonest gain. This is a personal transformation that leads to national transformation. Before we end this chapter, I want us to consider the farewell speech of the transformed disciple Paul to his followers. I have not coveted anyone's silver or gold or clothing, you yourselves know that these hands of mine have supplied my own needs and the needs of my companions. They all wept as they embraced him and kissed him, what grieved them most was his statement that they would never see his face again" (Acts 20:32–37).

Is it any wonder that such a profession and display of integrity and honesty provoked heartfelt loyalty from Paul's followers or that their grief was so great over the thought of losing Paul? If you left government—or any office, for that matter—would your followers grieve so openly about losing you, and if they did, would any of their grief relate to losing a leader of integrity? These are all the reasons why we are underdeveloped as a nation. The essence of transformation is to bring about an improvement in all areas of life while eliminating unwanted change. But this cannot happen in isolation. We need all Liberians—men, women, and children—to embrace truthfulness and be accountable for our actions at all times; it is time to refocus our attention to embrace the importance of national transformation.

CHAPTER 11

Occupational Distribution for National Recovery

Quickly, let us take a look at the occupational structure. According to encyclopedia.com (1998) occupational structure refers to the "aggregate distribution of occupations in society, classified according to skill level, economic function, or social status. There are 4 major factors that can or could impact the occupational structure of a nation, namely: "(1) the structure of the economy - the relative weight of different industries, (2) technology and bureaucracy - the distribution of technological skills and administrative responsibility, (3) the labour market- the pay and conditions attached to occupations, and (4) status and prestige - influenced by occupational closure, lifestyle, and social values."

These factors roles in developing the occupational structure are based on the changes a nation go through over the time.

One of the purposes of the national recovery is to shape the occupational structure at all levels for the expansion of both white-collar occupations and workers in various occupational classifications, including lawyers, doctors, nurses, sales personnel, tailors, market women, farmers, you name it. One fact to consider is that our nation is underdeveloped; therefore, work participation rate of the labor force is low. So what can the government do to boost the economic welfare of the country? There can be multiple answers to this question. First, the government can build a solid foundation for economic success and shared prosperity by investing in education. Providing expanded access to high-quality education will not only expand economic opportunity for the citizens but also strengthen the overall national economy. Second, the country can increase the strength of its economy and its ability to grow and attract high-wage employers by investing in education and increasing the number of well-educated workers. (Breger & Fisher, 2013). Third, the central government and the counties across the country should take a stand, realizing that they must take a more aggressive and expansive role in economic policy. And fourth, robust national education systems are good not just for the national economy but also for the citizens of the country.

Ultimately, national economic policies seek to improve the lives of the people in the nation, which means creating conditions in which people can get jobs that pay enough to support a family and provide economic security (Breger & Fisher, 2013). If we are to recover in this area, the government must create occupational security among the population with a more skilled and well-educated workforce; hence, this is a key to the nation's prosperity. If each citizen can have an occupation or a career, a process that the government can facilitate, Liberians will be able to earn a decent living, sustain their families and save for retirement. This occupational distribution is affected by these factors—the availability of our natural resources, the level of technological development, and the level of education.

There are lots of talented and gifted people with God-given potential and abilities that need to be encouraged by the government to bring out the best in them. They are the emerging and future leaders. If only they are given the opportunity and a proper working environment to exercise these abilities, they will do something meaningful with their lives. Leading people is not about enriching oneself; it is about empowering others and reflecting the true nature of a great leader whose aim is shaping the destiny of others as well as respecting the values and dignity of the people. Empowering the people will help them reach their fullest potential. When a nation cannot empower its people, then an occupational gap is created. There will not be enough professionals, and this creates a volume of professional vacancies, causing the government to import experts and other professionals who will become a financial burden. Imagine what Liberians could become if they are given the opportunity. Let us believe that the decades ahead will provide greater opportunities to people who will be able to touch every level of our society if the government progresses in this direction of closing the occupational gap.

Here is a logical question that I would like to ask: Are those of us who are Christians willing to be a part of the solution, or are we part of the problem? Surely you would like to know why these questions are asked. It can be proven that 95 percent of the workforce in this nation identifies as Christian, and there is still a high level of corruption in the workplaces. Based on this analysis, Christians in government are as much a part of the problem as anyone else. There is no difference in how the average Christian behaved as compared to non-Christians regarding trust and handling the resources entrusted to them for national development. Too often we Christians think that because we are Christian, we have the divine obligation to do just anything. We do have a divine duty to do the right thing. However, many Christians are violating basic principles of finance and human resources. Your credibility and integrity as a steward that never returns once lost. A divine platform of stewardship had been laid down for us. "In charge of the storehouses I appointed Shelemiah the priest, Zadok the scribe, and pedaiah of the Levites, and in addition to them was Hanan, the son of Zaccur, the son of Mattanian. They were considered reliable, and it was their task to distribute to their kinsmen" (Nehemiah 13:13). These were reliable men placed in charge to manage finances for the temple. Let us put this in a Liberian context now. They were given the responsibility to manage state funds for the development and advancement of the nation because they were spiritually, mentally, physically, and financially reliable. What do you think could be the result?

Permit me to say that it would have been the opposite of the account in this chapter in Nehemiah. The absence of reliable people in the Liberian government has shaped our economy and put us in a crippling condition, and this has caused unimaginable suffering and destruction to the society. The reality is that during the time of our independence, many of our leaders were occultists, involved in secret societies; the devil blinded them. Both military personnel and civilians have been very corrupt and involved in dishonest practices and lacking integrity in their commitment to the nation's progress. Our leaders fight for their benefits, their insatiable greed, for riches, their desire to gain and hoard wealth. This has created a bad situation that is depicted in the scriptures. Hosea

9:9 says, "They have gone deep in depravity as in the days of Gibeah; He will remember their iniquity, He will punish their sins." Isaiah 1:4 says, "Alas, sinful nation, people weighed down with iniquity, Offspring of evildoers, Sons who act corruptly! They have abandoned the Lord they have despised the Holy One of Israel they have turned away from Him." Proverbs 20:4 says, "The sluggard does not plow after autumn, so he begs during the harvest and has nothing." The last scripture helps us understand that when we do not put our time to use while there is time, we become beggars and liabilities on other people. This is why our leaders have to strategically start planning now and responsibly do everything to the best of their abilities; they can leave a powerful legacy behind for the future generations to bring about the change for occupational distribution and national recovery.

We need a total change of leadership that will bring change to the nation. In music we call this modulation, transitioning from one key to another; likewise, we need to change the nation's mood and create a different environment. We must open the door to the study of different areas and professions: conducting experiments and research to obtain knowledge of the natural resources that God has so blessed us with. The University of Liberia, the state-owned institution of higher learning, should aim at redesigning its curriculum that will meet the standards and demands of modernity instead of just building students' lives around politics. Researcher Henry Mintzberg of McGill University stated, "Organizational effectiveness does not lie in that narrow-minded concept called rationality. It lies in the blend of clearheaded, logic, and powerful intuition. Discernment enables a leader to see a partial picture, fill in the missing pieces intuitively, and find the real heart of a matter." We can't just create any kinds of job and mockery professions just so that people can get by accidentally. A situation like this makes a person malfunction. If we are true to ourselves, we will come to understand why many of our population are counterproductive, disadvantageous, and profitless to the society. This is why our government needs to build and develop the lives of its citizens around specialized technological and industrial areas with the necessary skills and abilities to make them competent and competitive to meet the challenges occupational distribution in relations to national recovery.

CHAPTER 12

National Recovery for Standard of Living

Before we begin with this topic, let us define the phrase "standard of living." The standard of living refers to the extent to which individuals (Liberians) or families can satisfy their needs. This indicates the volume of available resources, goods, and services at the disposal of its citizens and therefore shows the level of their well-being. A person who enjoys a better life is said to have a high standard of living, and this is what all Liberians are yearning for. It means that the people can afford to enjoy a great variety of things in the nation. The standard of living for Liberians will be a reflection of the kind of leaders we will have in the new Liberia. Primarily, we can say that the standard of living is how well or how poorly a person or group of people live in terms of having their needs and wants met (yourdictionary.com). An example of a high standard of living is a wealthy person who can afford anything he or she wants as compared to a low standard of living with a poor person who cannot afford or does not have enough food or water.

One major reason why a government exists is to create rules and provide law and order to protect and seek the well-being of people. Government responsibilities also extend to the economy and public services. During the 1960s, US president Lyndon Johnson unveiled his "great society" programs aimed at eliminating poverty in the entire country, and it is still working today in America. The Liberian government has the responsibility to provide the parameters for everyday activities and create programs for its citizens that will enhance their living standard. The Unity Party government came up with a deceitful scheme referred to as the "Poverty Reduction Strategy

(PRS)" that sunk the entire country into economic depression, while most of our government officials transferred huge amounts of money to America to buy houses to support their families and concubines at the detriment of the Liberian people. A very wise political scientist named Dr. Manwoo Lee said "that the government has three responsibilities to its citizens— (1) ensuring access to education (libraries, schools, etc.), (2) ensuring access to safety (health care, security, firefighting, etc.), and (3) providing safeguards for the environment (protecting our wildlife and national forests)". Also, President Thomas Jefferson once said, "The first and only objective of a good government is the care of human life and happiness and not their destruction." On the contrary, we are being destroyed economically by corrupt demagogues who want to leave us destitute in our current state by perpetuating a vicious cycle of misery. In actuality, the people are the government; we are the ones who choose our representatives to represent our best interests.

A study was done on Scandinavia showing the people are composed of a small and nearly homogeneous population, but they're a shining example of how "everyone takes care of one another" because the people are the government and the government is the people. But you can see the loopholes and how devastating it has become in our own country. We expect the government to take up their responsibility for the welfare of its citizens. The citizens are what makeup Liberia, so to keep Liberia together, the government first has to make sure that its citizens are in good living condition. The representatives are there to guide the interest of the people not to seek theirs.

There would be no government without the people, but our government officials are allowed to go unanswerable. It is said in ethics and governance "accountability is answerability, blameworthiness is reliability, and expectation is account-giving."

Now let's look at government accountability and see how we can recover economically. Government accountability means that public officials, whether elected or not, must explain their decisions and actions to the citizens. Further, government accountability is achieved through the use of a variety of mechanisms—political, legal, and administrative—designed to prevent corruption and ensure that public officials remain answerable and accessible to the people they serve. In the absence of such mechanisms, corruption may thrive (US Department of State).

There are no sanctions placed on these elected officials, and we don't currently investigate whether they have met the standards expected of them or not. Sanctions imply a process in which those charged with responsibilities are in some way punished for falling below the standard expected of them. This is the hell we're going through in this nation. There is an economic crisis going on. The economy is really in bad shape because of those greedy politicians. Did you know that greed is associated with idolatry? Colossians 3:5 says, "Therefore consider the members of your earthly body as dead to immorality, impurity, passion, evil desire, and (greed) which amount to idolatry." Jeremiah 6:13 says, "For from the least of them even to greatest of them, everyone is greedy for gain, and from the prophet, even to the priest everyone deals falsely." Luke12:15 says, "Then he said to them beware, and be on your guard against every form of greed; for not even when one has an abundance does his life consist of his possessions." II Peter 2:14 says, "Having a heart trained in greed, greed is the desire to have something more than is necessary." The issue of greed is affecting our leaders spiritually, physically, economically. Here is the root cause of the economic crisis we are experiencing. "Idolatry is the worship of idols; it is called idolism" (Bakr, n.d). This idea is woven deep into the fabric of our society, and it has severely damaged our nation. The worship of money as an idol is the same as the love of money, which is the root of evil. This desire has become one of the basic structures of our society, and this is a major reason for the low standard of living. Only the scriptures show us the root of what is happening. Jeremiah 6:13 says, "O that from the least the ordinary and poor people, to the greatest." The president, the legislature, the judiciary, those in government, every level of religion, prophets, and priests are greedy for gain. So, they deal falsely. That is corruption. People's hearts are trained in greed. People go to school, earn a degree, and become corrupt because they were trained to do so. Jesus said, "Beware and be on your guard against every form of greed." You see, we are to be on guard against greed like a watchman who keeps guard over the nation's resources to protect it from vandals and thieves; instead, we embraced every form of greed. This is why many people do not have a better standard of living. It is in the government's best interest for as many of its citizens as possible to be productive. Most of our leaders made no impact in this particular area to stand against greed, which is the mother of all forms of corruption. We need to stand up against this corrupt system. This is a system handed down to us by those who were before us. The Word of God says, "Blessed is the man who does not walk in the counsel of the wicked." This is not something imaginary. Government is making things worse for the ordinary people. I challenge any leader to cast the national recovery for a better standard of living as the vision for his or her campaign. People will follow you because they know you care. Forget about impressing people with empty words. Our government needs to refocus its attention on the people. Benjamin Franklin always thought of himself as an ordinary citizen. This was one of the secrets of his success.

Liberia is an emerging nation faced with the biggest economic crisis that is still affecting the living standard of the common people, and it needs a leadership that will seek ways to improve the lives of its citizenry. To achieve this, our government must be determined to give its undivided attention to the needs of the people. This book has identified the source of our problems for the government so that we can create plans to resolve them. People in governmental positions must reexamine and redefine the standard of living of the people for which they were elected to serve. People need a lead way to redirect their lives for the better. In this national recovery process, we need tenderhearted leaders, leaders who will show concern for the people like in Jeremiah 9:1, which says, "Oh that my head were a spring of water; I would weep day and night for the slain of my people." That is the heart of a true leader. In securing an aspiring leader with this compassionate heart, we will take a significant step toward a peaceful accession.

Recovery means to restore the loss of hope. Some people are the sole surviving members of their families. They need hope to restore their lost dignity, lost identity, lost innovation, and lost creativity. Many nations, including ours, have inequity problem, and it is challenging to deal with all the inequities from a human standpoint. But John the Baptist asserted a statement for us to follow in Luke 3:11. "The man with two tunics should share with him who has none, and the one who has food should do the same." This is why we are admonished to be guarded against greed. A greedy man will not share; he hoards. He accumulates wealth at the expense of others. Some people have everything, but the principles of sharing make no difference to them. To go a little further, it is more blessed to give than to receive (Acts 20:35). One way to improve the standard of living of the people is to provide an affordable means of education, create jobs, and provide fair working conditions with a set minimum wage.

When a government takes power, many people depend on them for a better livelihood. With a good visionary in a leadership role, I believe Liberians can become productive, organize, and build our infrastructure, and then we can take the world stage in marketing our achievements with respect to our abundant natural resources. When you show people their worth and profitability, they become very creative. Liberians are looking for a leadership that will give them purpose and a livelihood at such a time when they do not know where to turn. Many times people come to power just to impress without compassion for the people. The prime motive of any leadership in this economic crisis should be in helping the people. Many people have been cut off and displaced out of their inheritance in Liberia because of greed and bad leadership. Let's see the kind of leadership that will make an impact on the lives of the people. II Samuel 9:7 says, "Don't be afraid, for I will surely show you kindness for the sake of your father Jonathan. I will restore to you all the land that belonged to your grandfather Saul and you will always eat at my table." This is a biblical example of recovery for our leaders to follow so that they can let their followers know they care. Jesus was one of the most caring leaders of all times.

In biblical times and in modern times, it is said that people enthusiastically followed leaders who care about them. The lack of this care has deepened the economic depression because our leadership has wrecked our economy by showing no mercy or care for the common people. True caring creates more loyalty to the leaders. Being insensitive to the well-being of others creates chaos in the land. To achieve national recovery is to change the standard of living for the masses. It is essential that people know that their leaders care about them in this time of deep economic crisis. Our leaders should realize that when people are treated poorly or their needs ignored, leadership is tarnished. National recovery calls for a sense of focus and prioritization. Without love and care in the new Liberia and a desire to see people lifted, we create a poor cohesion and a diluted sense of true national identity.

"The love of liberty brought us here." Empty rhetoric accomplishes nothing for the people. It is imperative that our elected officials understand that the primary beneficiaries of their collective caring are the citizens. One motto for a leader could be "I am committed to helping every Liberian obtain his or her dream." The climate at home often influences people, and you can reach them by lifting them to higher standards and showing them, you care. I believe it is essential that our leaders act prudently because the sooner we identify the problems, the sooner we can eliminate them and create the solutions. This is the kind of leadership we must anticipate to transform the living standard of the people in the new Liberia for national recovery. Greedy politicians created the economic mess we have now, and they expect the next generation to clean it up. They are responsible not only for the economy shutting down and collapsing but the collapse of the government as well.

They promised us that they knew about good governance and running an effective economy. On the contrary, we are at the stage of a deepening economic depression, affecting the standard of living of the common people. In this recovery process, the nation needs strong and sound leadership with credibility. Every president who takes the higher office has had a chief economic advisor, and yet look where we are today as a nation. Many of our people are not professionally and mentally prepared to handle this. To most Liberians, the economy is like a nightmare from which they are expecting to awaken at any moment. Economic crimes are becoming so rampant throughout the country, and they are breaking the Liberian society apart. Here is a clear picture in Matthew 25:12, which says, "If a kingdom is divided it cannot stand." It is a strong economy that will hold the nation together. I think this is an unprecedented move by greedy politicians in creating an unstable economy for us. We are looking for leaders who will revive and stabilize the economy. It is imperative then we understand that it is the degree of excellence that makes people better. We are created in the image of God. The standards God set from the beginning are the standard by which our standards are measured. We know those standards God is set for humankind through his Word in Genesis 1:28. "God blessed them, and God said to them, be fruitful and multiply, and fill the earth, and subdue it: and rule over the fish of the sea, and over the birds of the sky, and over every living thing that moves on the earth." From this verse of scripture, it can be realized that the deepest craving of mankind is to find a sense of significance and relevance regardless of his or her race, color, ethnic heritage, socioeconomic status, or nationality.

This need of significance is the cause of all the chaos, disorderliness, confusion, war, and destruction of lives and properties as well as the pervasive corruption in the land. Politicians do not care about the people who voted them into power. As I stated before, our leaders are just godless and greedy outlaws. The organization of a society should not be aimed at dominating, oppressing, or suppressing our fellow human beings. Corruption is a brutal system of theft that creates poverty and low standards of living for others. And this is what we have experienced over the years. This brutal system enables an elite person who comes to power to enrich himself and to own the means of control over others through politics. Liberians need to take a heroic stand to work with leaders who want to make a change. Sometimes it only takes one person to make a difference. Our leaders must make the sacrifice to ensure a high quality of life for their people. Elected officials should do everything within their power to minimize the impact of poverty on the lives of the people they represent. Your sacrifice can make success possible. Those representatives who are elected to manage the country's affairs should typically place a high premium on the living standard of the citizens. National goals must be set, and the goals must not be interrupted by self-important bureaucrats.

Our elected officials should know about the nature of government from a biblical perspective. Romans 13:1 points out that everyone must submit to the governing authority, for all authority comes from God and those who have been placed in positions of authority are put there by God. Therefore, our senators and representatives are representatives for the people and not themselves. They should better the lives of the people in their constituencies. If those handling our economy had not spent the country into poverty, we wouldn't be in this economic mess in the first place. With life in Liberia degrading for most people and violence escalating rapidly, we need better economic alternatives with decisive and innovative steps to survive the economic crisis. Let me insert an ideological principle of economics for our nation or otherwise. You cannot spend more than you make indefinitely, and this is exactly what our government officials are doing. Many of our unfortunate politicians have not discovered that what seems to make sense in a stable economy becomes nonsensical in a volatile economy. To recover nationally, we must apply biblical economic principles. It is the Word of God that governs our decisions, not the tricky ideas of man.

Many of our political leaders get educated abroad, especially in the great United States of America, and they acquire vast knowledge and lots of degrees. However, their knowledge and experience become worthless without the development of the social and economic fabric of the nation. There has also been a reduction in minerals and human resources. To achieve national recovery, our government must make it a priority to invest in human resources. With human being the key word here, my brothers and sisters this is the clear answer to this problem. Social capital should also be considered. "Social capital is defined as "the networks of relationship among people (Liberians) who live and work in a particular society (Liberia), enabling that society (Liberia) to function effectively (The Buddha's advice to Laypeople, 2017). This is the revelation made known to us in this book on how to recover nationally. Revelation reveals a surprising and previously unknown fact, especially one that is made known in a dramatic way.

Finally, this is not some philosophical or political issues we are dealing with. It is a Liberian issue and the future of a great nation and its people hidden in the grips of a few greedy and corrupt individuals.

CHAPTER 13

Avoid Consumer Mentality

The word consumes can mean "do away with completely" or "spend wastefully." For instance, when we read books, we do not refer to reading as consuming in that sense because they do not cease to exist after we have read them. They become a part of us and change us. A person who acquires goods and services for his or her own needs starts as a producer and not just a consumer. One way to find out about the effectiveness and productiveness of people is the mentality, whether a producer – one who create things or a consumer one who consume anything and everything. Every society has these two kinds of mentalities: consumer and producer. The consumers are those people have nothing to contribute to society while producers are innovative, creative, and productive. It is like the Word of God. When it abide in us, we become producers, givers, and not just consumers. John 15:5–8 says,

I am the vine, you are the branches; he who abides in me and I in him, he bears much fruit, for apart from me you can do nothing. If anyone does not abide in Me, he is thrown away as a branch and dries up; and they gather them, and cast them into the fire and they are burned. If you abide in me and my words abide in you, ask whatever you wish, and it will be done for you. My father is glorified by this, that you bear much fruit, and so prove to be my disciples.

An individual with a consumer mentality lives with self-pity; this is where most Liberians are today. It's like reverting to our childhood. Consumer mentality is affecting many people in this country. The nation is ruined when people just become consumers; this also causes incessant demands. People must engage the functions of their minds efficiently and profitably if we're to survive and be sustained as a nation. A man who works for a salary but lacks adequate control of his finances is highly vulnerable to substantial losses, thus making him a consumer who is always in a vacuum. The consumers just want to get by while the producer mentality possesses a dedication, leading them to produce high-quality work consistently and contribute to society.

Reliability is one of the words we can use to describe a person with a producer mentality. Because these people put effort into portraying and proving their dependability by being productive and contributing to society, their high level of productivity constitutes the primary ingredient of the people's well-being. The fact is that individuals like these appear more beneficial to the nation.

Character is also built into the producer's mentality. They are self-disciplined, pushing themselves to be outstanding and productive citizens; they are also often sincere and trustworthy. These traits become befitting and useful, distinguishing themselves from the rest. II Timothy 4:11 says, "Take Mark, and bring him with thee; for he is profitable to me for the ministry." People with a consumer mentality are not profitable to society. In practice, this means Liberia should constantly be assessing all of its people with potential and placing them where they can develop and make the maximum contribution to society.

As we're entering the recovery process, the nation's leaders must begin to realize that we can only develop and progress as a people as we avoid the consumer mentality. It is imperative that we put in place a system to assure the competency, purposefulness, and morality of top leaders in the new Liberia. We can have all the traits of leadership, but if we don't nationally promote the development of the producer mentality, the preparation for greatness and progressiveness will not be sustainable.

Liberians need mentors—mentors who will change the way the people think and help them make something of themselves. The people want to be protégés of leaders who have a producer's mentality and can offer them guidance when needed. The kind of relationship that is anticipated between protégés and their mentors should be reminiscent of Elijah and Elisha's in the Old Testament. When Elijah was about to be taken to heaven, he asked his protégé, "Elisha, tell me what can I do for you before

I am taken from you?" "Let me inherit a double portion of your spirit," Elisha replied (2 Kings 2:9). Elisha could have asked for anything—goods, prosperity, money, or a powerful position, as many would do today, but what he asked for is what mentors have the power to give to their protégés, the benefit of their anointing and life experiences.

To be a consumer is not all there is to life. You have a greater responsibility to transform your mentality to impact and leave a bigger footprint in making Liberia a great nation. Many people in this country feel no fulfillment in life because there is nothing to challenge them. People need innovation and motivation to add something more fulfilling to their lives and restore a sense of purpose. Our present condition as a nation with a consumer mentality does not determine the rest of our lives. Jabez is an obscure person mentioned in only two verses of scripture. In 1 Chronicles 4:9–10, he had a condition that many thought was permanent, but he broke through to a blessed life. Jabez shows us a principle to learn from. It's only what you believe will happen that will release God's power upon you and bring about a changed life. Jabez was more honorable than his brothers, and his mother named him Jabez, saying, "Because I bore him pain." Now Jabez called on the God of Israel, saying, "Oh that you would bless me indeed and enlarge my border, and that your hand might be with me, and that you would keep me from harm that it may not pain me (Chronicles 4:9–10). As requested in his prayer, God granted him what he prayed for. We want to ask God to enlarge our lives so we can make a greater impact for him and our nation. This is not for personal gain but a channel with opportunity and responsibility to make a mark for God in our nation and the world.

The name Jabez means "he causes pain." Those with a consumer mentality can assume that something about Jabez's birth was exceptionally more painful than a usual birth—either physically or emotionally. Being branded a person with a consumer mentality is painful because nothing good comes out of you like Jabez, a man with painful past and no hope for the future. Picture yourself in this story. You may be an individual struggling to find meaning and significance to life or a person who is desperate to be accepted by your peer because of your consumer mentality. Names were very important in the Bible those days. A name often defined a person's future, what they could become. Jabez's hopeless name and a dysfunctional beginning made him appear as if he had nothing to offer.

Before Italian explorer Christopher Columbus set sail from Spain in 1492 and stumbled upon the Americas, the Spaniards had prided themselves on their misinformed belief that their country was the last. Early Spanish coins were encrypted with the words Ne Plus Ultra, which is a Latin phrase meaning - No More Beyond. They believed there was nowhere else after Spain, and if one ventured into the endless sea, certain danger laid ahead (Anonymous, n.d.). Ne Plus Ultra, I believe are the same three words that have been stamped on the minds of those with a consumer mentality. Those who live in this country thinking that they cannot go beyond their self-imposed boundaries, who are accustomed to embracing the negative side of life and feeling that they are incapable of accomplishing anything worthwhile fall in the category of Ne plus Ultra. This consumer mentality has damaged and crippled lots of our brothers and sisters even in the diaspora. The consumer mentality makes one think, No more beyond this point of my life, No more political instability after another, and No more beyond the point of drug abuse and other self-destructive consumer goods, and the list goes on. You may be at the receiving end, always asking for alms. Alms refers to handouts, charitable donations, and begging for the reduction or cancellation of debt. This is the consumer mentality that has become a great fallacy that we need to change and avoid. As you read the keys to national recovery, do not allow the consumer mentality and its circumstances to get you off track.

We need the right attitude in this recovery process. Family life expert Denis Waitley addresses this issue "The winner's edge is not in a gifted birth, a high IQ, or in talent, the winner's edge is all in the attitude, not aptitude." It is an attitude that we need as a criterion to recover and succeed. Our attitude is very crucial in this season of national recovery because it determines how we think and act as a people. Today in our country, there are people in top leadership positions with negative attitudes. They do not understand that the people they lead are mirrors of their attitudes, either good or bad. The law of magnetism states that "who you are is who you attract." The consumer mentality is always coupled with a self-pity attitude. In Earth and Altar, Eugene H. Peterson wrote, "Pity is one of the noblest emotions available to human being, self-pity is possibly the most ignoble ... [It] is an incapacity, a crippling emotional disease that severely distorts our perception of reality ... a narcotic that leaves its addicts wasted and derelict." The more negative you are, the longer it will take to change the consumer mentality. The person with a consumer mentality is self-indulgent, dwelling on his or her sorrows or misfortunes which can lead to an inferiority complex and significantly impact one's well-being and the nation as well.

CHAPTER 14

Repairers of Wasted Lives

Currently, we have become a wasteful society. Many of us today have damaged the value of life with no purpose. People commit acts of flagrant destruction inconsistent with the fruitful use of their lives. God has a present and future purpose for our lives that will bring about some unique value. A wasteful life is a life without purpose. In the wisdom of God, he chooses to operate through people like you and me, struck down but not destroyed. In 2 Corinthians 4:8–9, the apostle Paul wrote, "We are afflicted in every way, but not crushed; perplexed but not driven to despair; persecuted, but not forsaken; struck down, but not destroyed."

In the movie Creed, boxer Adonis Creed takes a brutal punch in the fight of his life and gets knocked to the ground. He hits the floor hard. The people in his corner are shouting, "Get up! Get up!" His opponent is on the ropes, celebrating, thinking the fight is over. But while Creed is out, his mind is scrolling through all he is been through up until that point and all the people who love and motivate him. Like a jolt, he is up before the count of ten, and he's back in the fight (Tate, 2016). Creed's boxing life may seem to resemble our lives as a people. We have encountered many battles in life, and many of us are still recovering. So, you can get up. As with Creed, the enemy may be celebrating, thinking it is over when it is not over. Like Paul, you can say, "I can do all things through Christ who strengthens me (Philippians 4:13).

One biblical character who wasted his life was Samson. God created us to live for his glory. A wasted life is a life that is not lived for the glory of God. Individuals with wasted lives do not know why they were created because they live for their glory and their immediate satisfaction and not for the joy and benefits of others. Romans 3:23 says, "For all have sinned and fall short of the glory of God." The truth is that sin, as defined in the original translations of the Bible, means "to miss the mark." In this case, the mark is the standard of perfection established by God and evidenced by Jesus. People need biblical guidance, and so this book is my effort at biblical wisdom. Fathers should stop letting their children down and wasting their lives by indulging into extramarital affairs that cause disastrous and lasting damage.

Experts say children who learn about parental infidelity react similarly to children whose parents divorce, except the emotional responses to cheating are deeper and can have greater and longer-lasting impacts. Infidelity violates everything they know about their parents. Their parents have told them good things, told them the truth, and suddenly, they discover that their parent is doing something way outside the promises they know that their mom and dad have made to each other. Infidelity also damages an individual's confidence. Infidelity is a terrible disillusion, says one clinical psychologist. "To find out that one of my parents was profoundly dishonest to my other parent. And if they are so dishonest with the parent, why would they be more honest with their kids?" You begin to question the foundations of your relationship. Psalm 11:3 says, "If the foundations are destroyed what can the righteous do?" Many of our children do not know their fathers because they were never there for them while growing up. Children are like precious jewels. Diamonds are formed by pressure covered in dirt, but when you polish them, they shine (Anonymous, n.d.).

We have to see the shine in our children. This is what makes us repairers of wasted lives, restoring that luster. We are created not to waste our lives. Let us consider how the events of Samson's wasted lifestyle affected his future. Like many of us, Samson never got past his past. We are supposed to decide not to let our past dictate our future. A man of God said, "Let your past refine you and not define you." It may have been late for Samson, but it is not late for you. Many of us wasted our lives and became enslaved to sin. When we surround ourselves with the wrong people, who cannot bring fulfillment to our lives because the wrong will bring the wrong. God opened my eyes to something in Judges 16:30 "And Samson said, 'Let me die with the Philistines,' and he bent with all his might so that the house fell on the lords and all the people who were in it." When we live without purpose and waste our lives, our lives do not benefit ourselves and others. Why? Because those lives are attached to us. I Samuel 22:2 says, "Everyone who was in distress, and everyone who was in debt, and everyone who was discontented gathered to him; and he became captain over them." Now there were about four hundred men with him. Those men's lives depended on David. Without him, their lives would have been meaningless. He gives them purpose and identity. Samson renewed his purpose, but only at his death. He was blinded, shattered, scourged, and mocked, but God restored his strength. God is restoring us, but we must understand that restoration is usually gradual as we can see from the restoration of Samson's hair.

Restoration comes as we release our old ways, habits, and deeds, allowing God to rebuild our lives and our decision-making ability slowly. Today many of us are ashamed and full of regrets and despair because of the life we have lived. However, even Samson trusted God for one last time. Instead of dying the hero God created him to be, he died blind at the mercy of other people. This is a powerful example of us today. We are at the mercy of other people. We are all born with incredible potential and great expectation, but strings of bad choices and decisions led us where we are today. Sometimes parents look to their children for support, but they are let down when the children cannot supply those needs. We must understand that the whole of Israel depended on Samson for deliverance, but the children of Israel were let down. When we are born, we look like our parents, but when we die, we look like our choices. Samson died the way he died because of his choices. So, we need to refocus. We need to get our lives back. We need to believe that God can bring us significance, power, and meaning and make our lives count as He intended. Your life and my life both belong to God, and therefore, he knows what life is for. The only way to avoid living a wasted life is to let God lead.

Our lives are in his hands. Job 12:10 says, "In whose hand is the life of every living thing, and the breath of all mankind." Your life does not consist in the abundance of things or your possessions. Life is not the accumulation of things Luke 12:15 says, "Then He said to them, 'Beware, and be on your guard against every form of greed; for even when one has an abundance does his life consist of his possessions.'" Luke 12:16–21 says,

And He told them a parable, saying, "The land of a rich man was very productive, and he began reasoning to himself, saying, 'What shall I do, since I have no place to store my crops?'" Then he said, "This is what I will do; I will tear down my barns and build larger ones, and there I will store all my grain and goods, And I will say to my soul, 'Soul, you have many goods laid up for many years to come; take your ease, eat, drink and be merry,'" But God said to him, "You fool, This very night your soul is required of you; and now who will own what you have prepared?" So is the man who stores up treasure for himself, and is not rich toward God.

This is what is happening to lots of people in this country. They live wasted lives by just piling up wealth because they think that's what life is all about.

The story begins with the land of a wealthy man who was very productive. Picture Liberia as a productive land, but because of greed and selfishness, we are underdeveloped. We have lots of fools in this country who are storing up money and calling themselves rich, but when you look in the realm of the spirit, God addresses them as fools. Many of us have gifts and talents and businesses that bring us money, but life is not about accumulating things just for ourselves. Many foolish people who are on their death beds do not find comfort in their possessions. Comfort comes from the ability to say, "I have lived a life well spent." Deuteronomy 32:39 says, "See now that I, I am He, and there is no god besides me, It is I who put to death and give life, I have wounded, and it is I who heal, and there is no one who can deliver from My hand." I heard about a sign hanging in a man's kitchen that reads, "Only one life that will soon be past, only what's done for Christ will last." Matthew 16:24–25 says, "Then Jesus said to his disciples 'If anyone wishes to come after me, he must deny himself, and take up his cross and follow. For whoever wishes to save his life will lose it: but whoever loses his life for my sake will find it.'"

There was also a story about a seventy-eight-year-old man who came to an evangelistic meeting. When he heard the evangelist preach, he started to weep and weep and weep, and all he could say was, "I wasted, wasted, wasted my life." Does that sound like you, my friend? If this story identifies you, then God is speaking to you right now. He says this again in Matthew 16:26, which states, "For what will it profit a man if he gains the whole world and forfeits his soul? Or what will a man give in exchange for his soul?" This was Moses's choice, written in the book of Hebrews, concerning materialism, fame, popularity, and the treasures of Egypt. Hebrews 11:25–26 says, "Choosing rather to endure ill-treatment with the people of God than to enjoy the passing (pleasures) of (sin), considering the reproach of Christ greater riches than the (treasures) of Egypt; for he was looking to the reward. Let us examine these three words very carefully." We want to put them in order for our understanding—treasures, pleasures, and sin. These were the steps that the rich fool took. He forsook God in favor of riches. First, he began reasoning, saying, "What shall I do since I have no place to store my goods now?" This is someone who is obsessed with treasure. This is describing a person whose motive is dictated by money. Then he said, "This is what I will do. I will tear down my barns and build larger ones, and there I will store all my grain and my goods." Second, he is consumed by pleasure. "And I will say to my soul, 'Soul, you have many goods laid up for many years to come. Take your ease." Third, he's taken over by sin. He says, "Eat, drink, and be merry." Also, everything was about himself. This was a wasted life, and the result was, therefore, "You fool, this very night your soul is required of you; and now who will own what you have prepared? Salt is good, but if even salt has become tasteless, with what will it be seasoned? It is useless either for the soil or for the manure pile; it is thrown out, He who has ears to hear, let him hear" (Luke 14:34–35).

Do you have ears to hear God speaking to you as you read this book? There is one life to live, and we must live it well. I believe this message is targeting you and is speaking directly to your needs and wants to give understanding on the emotional and cognitive level. God wants us to see the urgency and applicability of a course of action from the message in this book. The message about repairing wasted lives through this national recovery needs to be more accessible to potential readers and to inspire all Liberians to overcome the odds and realize their heroic mission. Despite the increasing domination and devastated lives in the country, if and only if you dare be different, you could bring about a new paradigm shift that could spur radical change in many lives. Paul's instructions to his young subordinate Timothy shows perseverance. "I give you this charge; preach the word; be prepared in season and out of season; correct, rebuke, and encourage—with great patience and careful instructions" (2 Timothy 4:2–3).

We want to prepare the nation for greatness. Nations are people. If the people's lives are wasted, they cannot be great. Your changed life and my changed life will fuel progress toward the goal. Jesus said that he who has an ear to hear. Let him hear. Are you listening? The Bible is full of people who did not listen. Lot's wife did not listen to the warning not to look back at the burning cities of Sodom and Gomorrah, so she wound up as a pillar of salt. Pharaoh did not listen to Moses, not even after his nation was hit with ten catastrophic plagues. Noah, on the other hand, was a man who saw and understood the value of listening. God had to break someone like me before I started listening. Of course, it is not easy to listen when things are going well or in your favor.

People who live wasted lives do things before listening, and that is a total reverse of life Proverbs 18:13 says, "He who answers before listening—that is his folly and his shame." That is why so much shame and disgrace is upon the land. The word folly means foolish. Keys to National Recovery is intended to put us on the right path because many Liberians are on a journey to nowhere. Most often our leaders will ignore well-intentioned advice that could save this country and people from tremendous suffering. Like Samson, who was not listening felt in the trap of Delilah "She said, 'The Philistines are upon you Samson,' And he awoke from his sleep and said, 'I will go out as at other times and shake myself (free),' but he did not know that the LORD had departed from him" (Judges 16:20). So you see that a wasted life is a life that God has left or departed from. When people's lives are wasted incredibly, it is an indication of the kind of leadership that they have had. Jesus was addressing the Pharisees, who were the leaders in Israel at the time when He said in Matthew 15:14, "Let them alone; they are blind guides of the blind, and if a blind man guides a blind man, both will fall into a pit." At a certain age or in a certain condition you may feel you have wasted a lot of time. You are wondering if it is too late for you to achieve something worthwhile.

Our focuses are on the urgency of not wasting the days of our lives. We all make mistakes and regret our past. We have things that, if we had our own way, we would go back and change. In this case, God urges us to repent, but our society tells us to indulge in sin. The only hope for any individual or any society is to hear the Word of God and obey it. This is God's cry to us. Psalm 81:11–16 says,

But My people did not listen to My voice, And Israel did not obey Me, So I gave them over to the stubbornness of their heart, to walk in their own devices, Oh that my people would listen to Me, that Israel would walk in My ways, I would quickly subdue their enemies and turn My hand against their adversaries, Those who hate the LORD would pretend obedience to Him, And their time of punishment would be forever, But I would feed you with the finest of the wheat, And with honey from the rock I would satisfy you.

Psalm 11:3 also says, "If the foundation be destroyed, what can the righteous do?"

This passage symbolizes the importance of foundation. The leaders are the foundation of the nation. When the leaders are strong, the country is secured at the foundation. Nobody wants to live in a country that is designed to destroy his or her potential, or that is not interested in the development of its people. I believe that this will change. Our government tried to run us down. They even tried to frustrate us by killing our creativity, gifts, and talents and by stealing our intellectual property. Despite all the odds, I still love this country. This country has birthed many gifted people—George Oppong Weah, James Salinsa Debbah, Miatta Fahnbulleh, Marron D. Cassell, just to name a few. There are a few people who have made a great impact on my life. One was the late Fred Vamboo Boe Smith, Sr., who reminded me daily of my true purpose in life as a musician and provided encouragement for the development of music in Liberia. Papa Smith, Sr., saw young and talented people from the streets and took them through the process of training to become great musicians. He will always be known as the "Godfather of Liberia's Entertainment Industry" from the 1970s and 1980s. There were no institutions in Liberia at the time where one could cultivate artists to showcase their talents for the entertainment business. We want to remember him for the role he played in revolutionizing music and financially supporting young and talented groups. He was a cultivator and developer of musicians.

Another is Tonieh E. Williams, who brought dignity, quality, excellence, and professionalism and provided inspiration and purpose in the music industry. He had a dream for Liberia and felt he could express it through music. He also believed in the massive shift from limitation to the boundaries of possibilities. He formed the musical group popularly known as The Liberian Dream, which made the famous hit song "OAU Welcome to Liberia." These people were very instrumental in developing our gifts and talents. Because of their efforts, we could go places and expose our gifts and talents to other cultures. With the eyes of faith, I see a new Liberia with a new mentality. It is against this background that we shall examine what needs to be done to recover individually and nationally.

CHAPTER 15

Youth Empowerment

According to Wikipedia, youth empowerment is a process where children and young people are encouraged to take charge of their lives. They do this by addressing their obstacles, and then they take action to improve their situations. They transform their consciousness through their beliefs, values, and attitudes by the special grace of God. Let us see if we can decode this definition and break it down for our understanding. First, they need to be encouraged. The Greek word for encourage is parakaleo. It means you are giving someone support or confidence. It also means that you are helping to develop something in the person. Joshua was given a huge task as a youth—to lead the children of Israel through the wilderness to the Promised Land through enemies territory. Joshua becomes dismayed. God shows up to bring out the best in Joshua by encouraging him. In Joshua 1:6, God says, "Be strong and courageous, for you shall give this people possession of the land which I swore to their fathers to give them." It is our responsibility to encourage the youth in the society to bring out the best in them. Our government should provide programs that will help to empower the young people because they play an important part in shaping any society. I believe if youth empowerment is implemented on a national and individual level, the outcome could be very impactful. The ministry of youth and sports is the ministry through which the young of this country could build a better life for tomorrow. Building the life of the youth is very important because they are the ones who will be in government and private sector to functions in the country's tomorrow. If the youth are encouraged and empowered, Liberia's future prosperity will be secured.

We must ensure that this is done by the popular saying "The young people are the leaders of tomorrow."

Therefore, youth empowerment can also contribute to reducing the poverty rate in our communities and nation. If the youth are empowered with professional skills, they can use those skills to invest in their future and help others. The Ministry of Youth and Sports must get involved with the youths at all cost and levels to secure the nation's future. One of the biggest problems that we are facing in this nation involves the education sector. We expect those who received some level of education to be advocates for public education. The government has never focused or prioritized education in this nation; consequently, we see little children selling in our streets during school hours, and the government sits complacently. The United States that we look at as our model does not encourage such behavior. In fact, in a 1786 letter to George Wythe, Thomas Jefferson remarked, "The most important bill in our whole code is that for the diffusion of knowledge among the people." He believed that no other sure foundation can be devised for the preservation of freedom and happiness and not providing public education would leave the people in ignorance.

Empowering the youth of this country academically, I believe, will promote, and accelerate the spirit of patriotism through our education sector. My advice to those in the education sector is to provide massive scholarship programs for our youth. To those who are educated understand the power and value of the education you have received; therefore, it is incumbent upon you to provide and to support quality education for the next generation. If we deny educational empowerment to our youth, we deny our national recovery and the possibility of becoming great. Evidently, this is how the young people are going to meet the challenges and demands of society. The National Port Authority is not the gateway to the nation's economy, as it is often said—it is only being run as the gateway for high-level corruption and embezzlement. Frederic Bastiat, a French economist in the nineteenth century, said, "When plunder becomes a way of life for a group of men living together in a society, they create for themselves in the course of time a legal system that authorizes it and a moral code that glorifies it." Did you know that the gateway to the nation's economy is the people? Let us consider America, a nation with great people, great minds; they are the heroes of empowerment, especially youth empowerment. As a man thinks in his mind so is he (Proverbs 23:7). It is the people who make America's economy great—the business people, musicians, athletes, movie actors, doctors, just to name a few. This why many gifted and talented Liberians fleet home to contribute to the economy of that great nation. We can say because of no empowerment programs, youths that are eager to express their gifts and talents are emigrating to other nations. Thus Liberia is becoming a brain drain. Therefore, we need to start empowering our youth now so they can think great and serve greatly.

One of the things that serves as a stumbling block to youth empowerment is the issue of embezzling public funds by our government officials who are clothed with the responsibilities of setting an example of integrity. Thus, making the young people understand the danger of embezzling public funds because the future belongs to them. Today many of our young people are wasting away and are involved in all kinds of criminal activities, and our government has not realized that these youths need to be encouraged and empowered. We must empower them from the early stages to fight crime, to love their nation, and be the example to others. While I was writing this book, I discovered that one of the best ways to fight crime is through youth empowerment. It is the formula or solution.

The youth need to be empowered morally, academically, and financially to take the destiny of the nation into their hands. If the youth are not encouraged and empowered, there is a tendency to get discouraged and drift into other things. I used the word drift because there is nothing to guide them or inspire them. If nothing is inspiring and innovative for them to do, they might amount to nothing and become a burden to society. Study on Nwankwo Kanu, one of Nigeria's top footballers, who played for the Nigerian national team, as well as Portsmouth, Milan, Arsenal, Ajax, and West Bromwich Albion today has many heart treatment hospitals (known as Heart to Heart) in Nigeria. He sponsored these in appreciation for the support that the nation gave him during his football career. Wow! And who takes the credit? Nigeria, of course. After all, they empowered him.

We should also consider the security sector as a way of empowering youth. Youth empowerment in the security realm can provide national defense and protection. God also recognizes the value of the young people in his plan and divine purpose. They have desires; their hearts are filled with a vision of and for the future. Indeed, they are the most valuable asset to society. That is why the devil will make sure he damages the youth from the very foundation. "If the foundation be destroyed, what can the righteous do?" (Psalm 11:3). "Let no man despise your youth; but you be an example to the believers in, speech, conduct, love, faith and purity" (1 Timothy 4:12).

Every politician in this nation is supported by different interest groups all over the country, and this has always been true. The problem now is those political interests groups are not focused on the youth empowerment rather political interest. The danger is that those interests groups are so opposed to one another that they help prevent any meaningful thought about the young people of this country. Because in all their political infighting and cut-throat maneuvering, they serve their self-interests, while the best interests of the youth are being ignored. These overly ambitious politicians—though less principled in character—are reaching far more for themselves without stressing the needs of the next generation.

The youth needs to be empowered to understand the rule of law. People often say that they would compromise the law for the sake of peace, but the rule of law is necessary for a self-governing citizen. If we do not empower our youth in the area of law and order, we will only have ourselves to blame. Why is our focus on the youth within this particular topic? Good question. Let us get a view from our Creator's perspective. Proverbs 22:6 says, "Train up a child in the way he should go, even when he is old he will not depart from it." That is God's divine strategy for empowering the youths in every area. Why is Liberia the way it is? I believe it is due to the breakdown of law and order by the youth from what they learn from the older ones. Now consider the view of John Adams. He focused on setting up a constitution and a set of laws that would last as the American republic. He said, No man will contend that a nation can be free that is not governed by fixed laws, all other government than that of permanent, known laws is the government of mere will and pleasure (Watkins, 2016)." This paints a sobering picture of our government. He goes on to say; Permanent law has to be above the control of men who holds office under it (Waltkins, 2016). He also quoted Cicero, "Laws as, founded on eternal morals, they are emanations of the Divine Mind." The people should submit to the authority not of some imperfect human legislator but to the eternal legislator of the universe. Law is bound up with virtue, wisdom, religion, and morality. He said, "God made men for liberty (Watkins, 2016)." We can all bring national recovery through established laws and order. The youth needs help—your help, my help, and most especially, the government's help. Our Constitution provides delegation of power in which the legislature writes laws, the executive executes laws, and the judiciary interprets laws. Therefore, these branches of government clothed with authority to create and enforce laws that will govern youth empowerment.

So as we get on the way to national recovery, there should be a youth-focused campaign put in place so that the potential, abilities, and talents of the youth can be harnessed and utilized. This will enable the voice of the youth to be heard. We should include young people in the national recovery process. The leadership of the youth begins today. If they do not take the steps to leadership now, they may want to get there by bullets or force. There is a saying that goes, "The youth are the future's leaders." But the future begins from right where they are. The government should elevate the young people in this country. Those in leadership positions can set a national goal for the youth until it is achieved; Then, and only then will we be sure about those we call future leaders. We must express our concern for the youth. We must empower them in the new Liberia because they have great desires and great expectations. We do not want pay lip service to their plight because many times the youth are misunderstood and looked down upon. For us to claim that the future belongs to the youth is not enough. It will be more meaningful to remind the young people that they bear a special responsibility toward shaping their future. Their present is intimately related to their future, which will determine their future conditions and will reflect on their leadership. The youth in Liberia are destined for greatness, so our responsibility as the older generation is to make sure that we help them succeed and make admirable efforts to build a brighter future for them. Jeremiah 1:4–8 says,

Now the word of the LORD came to me, saying, "Before I formed you in the womb I knew you, and before you were born I consecrated you; I appointed you a prophet to the nations," Then I said: "Ah, Lord God, Behold, I do not know how to speak, for I am only a youth." But the LORD said to me, "Do not say, I' am only a (youth), for to all to whom I send you, you shall go, and whatever I command you, you shall speak. Do not be afraid of them, for I am with you to deliver you, declares the LORD."

Ecclesiastes 12:1 says, "Remember also your Creator in the days of your (youth) before the evil days come and the years draw near of which you will say, 'I have no pleasure in them.'"

You see, God has plans for the youth. We should also have a national vision for the youth by making them a new generation of great leaders. The youth are faced with many challenges in this country where mediocrity reigns. We must have great admiration for all youth and confidently affirm that they will make a massive difference. Liberian youths need the immediate attention of leaders who understand their value and the impact that education can have on a society. They represent the future, and so we look forward to their positive contributions in the future. Webster's Dictionary defines the word value as "that which is desirable, or worthy of esteem for its own sake; a thing or a quality that has intrinsic or inherent worth." That's our youth, and that is how we should picture them in the new Liberia.

For modern Liberian leaders, there should be a burning desire to formulate a clear and compelling agenda for the youths. II Peter 5:2–3 says, "Shepherd the flock of God among you, exercising oversight not under compulsion, but voluntarily, according to the will of God; and not for sordid gain, but with eagerness. Nor yet as lording it over those allotted to your charge, but proving to be examples to the flock." Let us examine the word sordid. It means "selfish, self-seeking, or mercenary." Mercenary means working or acting merely for money or other rewards – this means when people in leadership are mercenary, they are only interested in the money they can get from a particular situation. The reason many of our youths have nothing to commit themselves to is that the leaders themselves are committed to nothing. This is a simple depiction of our government officials who are supposed to be leading by example. McElroy of USAir spoke of commitment and its importance like this: "Commitment gives us new power; no matter what comes to us—sickness, poverty, or disaster—we never turn our eye from the goal." I think this is what the youths are anticipating—a goal, something to look forward to. Why are we not in the hallmark of great achievers? It is because commitment always precedes achievement. So there must be a goal set by the leaders for the youth to commit to. The Law of Buy-In by John C. Maxwell states, "People buy into the leaders, then the vision." Understanding this law requires that our leaders live exemplary lifestyles that are worthy of imitation. It will require street cred to lead others. Your position as a president or government representative is not enough to lead people who have been historically and systemically denied access to better opportunities. You cannot raise your sons and daughters in America while those you lead raise their sons and daughters in the ghettos like new Kru Town and West Point in Liberia out of gross negligence. The equality among the youths as citizens is essential to the progress of our nation. Let us look into the prophetic word and examine the leadership style of King David. First Chronicles 18:14 says, "So David reigned over all Israel, and he administered justice and righteousness for all his people." Let us paraphrase this verse of scripture and apply it to our situation. So the president reigned over all of Liberia and administered justice and righteousness for all the people. This is a biblical principle that we must follow if we are going to succeed as a nation by God's command.

There is a phrase in our national anthem that says. "Long live Liberia, happy land, a home of glorious liberty by God's command." If this glorious land of liberty was commanded by God, then change must be done God's way. This is the difference between our success and failure as a nation. Let us define the words justice and righteousness in the context of Liberia and our alignment with God's command for our leaders. Justice is fairness in the way that people are treated. Equality is equal status, rights, and responsibilities for all members of a society, group, or family. Righteousness promotes and makes a nation great. Proverbs 14:34 says, "Righteousness exalts a nation, but sin is a disgrace to any people." Therefore, so many indignities and injustices are present in our land. Proverbs 20:7 says, "A righteous man who walks in his integrity—how blessed are his sons after him." So leaders set the pace. For people to be blessed and empowered, the national leaders must set standards. If people keep pace with someone who is changing, they too change in response to that person. This is what it means to follow a pattern. The youth are our hope for tomorrow. We need to shape and design the Liberia that we will pass on to our successors. The government must set out several principles to guide the youth as successors. This is what great leaders do.

Let us consider one of the prime examples of a great leader. David was a generational thinker. In 1 Chronicles 21:5, David said, "My son Solomon is young and inexperienced, and the house that is to be built for the LORD shall be exceedingly magnificent, famous and glorious throughout all the lands. Therefore, now I will make preparations for it." So David made ample preparations before his death. Wow! This is real leadership. Let us say that David represents our government and Solomon represents the youths. The youths are young and inexperienced. The house to be built for the Lord represents the nation, which should be exceedingly magnificent, famous, and glorious through all the lands. This represents the beauty and greatness throughout every length and breadth of the nation. Every government needs to make ample preparations before relinquishing power to any newly elected government. This will also inspire and motivate the people like a legacy handed down to the next generation. It reminds me of our national anthem, which says, "Great be her fame, exceedingly magnificent famous, glorious land of liberty."

David did not just speak rhetorically like most of our leaders; he implemented the vision he had for the house of the Lord. The latter part of verse 5 says, "David made ample preparations before his death." It is a representation of a government that is transitioning, but before that, they made provisions for the next generation to carry on what they had projected for the future.

I believe when the leaders create an inspiring and inspirational goal for the youths to see, they will embrace it and run with it. This will create the passion and challenges for the youths to succeed. I encourage our elected officials to offer the national youth goals that will change this nation for good. When our leaders dedicate themselves to the goals they set, wonderful things will happen. When our government put taxpayer money to gainful goals to unify the efforts of the thousands of youths in this recovery process, life will become meaningful and hopeful. The future we dream of can become a reality. If the youths are given the opportunity, they can contribute tremendously and meaningfully to the progress and development of our society. A youth who is empowered has a specific role to play in achieving the goals that are set among their peers.

Daniel was a youth in the Babylonian system, which is much like ours today, but he had an unshakeable standard. Daniel 1:8 says, "But Daniel made up his mind that he would not defile himself with the king's choice food or with the wine which he drank; so he sought permission from the commander of the officials that he might not defile himself." Daniel made up his mind and acted upon his decision. I think the youths are Daniel's modern counterparts. They will define for themselves what they stand for. To be empowered, you must codify your goals and embrace a sustainable national goal. Codification refers to "a set of rules or goals you define and present in a clear and orderly manner." This could be described remarkably as the power of common goals for the youths. They will become participants, something larger than themselves. If the goal that is set is worthwhile, it will empower them individually and collectively. This effort will weave together the fabric of the new Liberia. The youth must value themselves to be of value to others. The Bible says, "They saw themselves as grasshoppers in their own sight so they were in their sight." This is referred to as the grasshopper mentality (i.e., a small view of yourself). You may see yourself as insignificant and unimportant, You may feel inferior, and you may perceive everything that is happening in your life as a reflection of what you cannot do or what you cannot be; however, you are pricelessly valued, and the contribution you make will be irreplaceable in your generation. But you must first readjust the image of yourself so that you have a godly perspective like David in Acts 13:36, which says, "For David, after he had served the purpose of God in his own generation, fell asleep, and was laid among his fathers and underwent decay."

Remember that in a postwar and broken-down nation like ours, you have been chosen in this season, unlike Gideon, who saw himself as nothing, inferior, frustrated, unmotivated, and unimportant. Then God said to him, "You mighty man of valor." This is what God is saying to you right now as you are reading this book. God is preparing you for greatness so that you can be productive and advance in education. Like Gideon, we live in an uncomfortable and intimidating society, but we must remain encouraged. The word encouraged means "to make (someone) more determined, hopeful, or confident." Your story is changing. When God speaks and you respond accurately by faith, your life can never be the same. You, a young man of valor, you can make it. Your determination and commitment to this national recovery process will make you an achiever. Be the hope of your peers today. You are the one being prepared for greatness within the nation. You make the nation great by being great yourself. Greatness has a starting place, and it all begins with you. Proverbs

23:7 says, "As a man thinks in his heart, so is he." You see, my friends, nobody will think for you. You will have to think for yourself. This means you can only change your environment by changing your thoughts. Develop a new way of thinking, and believe God for a new Liberia.

You have the capacity to create a new destiny in your generation and make a significant impact on those around you. You can stand as a reference point. You can move from a victim of society to a victor of society. I challenged you to break away from that destructive cycle of a lack of achievement, depravity, and ignorance. You are the ones to be celebrated and not just tolerated. You can reset your life right now by actively engaging in meaningful purposes and changing the negative thoughts about yourself. In 1 Corinthians 13:11, Paul says, "When I was a child, I used to speak like a child, think like a child, reason like a child; when I became a man, I did away with childish things." But who are your childish friends who have no purpose in life and are still giving you childish advice? I Corinthians 15:33 says, "God has given me advice for you great man, do not be deceived; bad company corrupts good morals." Proverbs 13:20 says, "He who walks with the wise men will be wise, but the companion of fools will suffer harm." Does that sound good? Certainly not. We are known by the company we keep. God wants to pull you away from the crowd. You need to choose and guard your circle of influence. Therefore, we are exhorted by the Word of God to come out from among them. But look at what Solomon's son, Rehoboam, did. I Kings 12:8 says, "But he forsook the counsel of the elders that they had given him, and consulted with the young men who grew up with him and served him." You need to start thinking big about your nation and yourselves. In the eyes of God, the youth must fulfill their prophetic destiny, and this must be the primary focus of the government. We must equip the future leaders (youth) of tomorrow.

The season has arrived for the youth to understand the responsibilities and challenges they are confronted with. Listen, God has given you talents and abilities to reflect his image. If you apply these principles, you will have an appointment with your God-given destiny. Welcome to your Future Foundation. You cannot afford to abort the leader in you that God intended you to be. God created you for a purpose. The most damaging thing for a youth is to walk with a crowd that would destroy his or her aspirations for the future.

Our elected officials have a huge task to start investing in the future of the youth. It is imperative in this season that they do not become a burden to society but instead become the new generation of leaders that will make life better for others. You will make an impact by committing to the goals you have set. The talent and gifts that God has placed in you can create the potential for greatness. But without commitment, your gifts and talents will be meaningless. I want you to know that the limitations you are faced with are self-imposed. Philippians 4:13 says, "I can do all things through Christ who strengthens me." I leave you with these encouraging words from NBA legend Michael Jordan. He explains, "Heart is what separates the good from the great." "As a man thinks in his heart so is he" (Proverbs 23:7).

CHAPTER 16

Create the Right Environment

How can we create the right environment for our intuition to improve? We must make a conscious decision to encourage innovation. Primarily, innovation needs a conducive atmosphere in which to develop; it is a cultural characteristic that we must encourage and nurture in our nation. People need a motivating environment, and motivation is developed by caring, not by scaring people. Scaring creates resentment as well as a lack of enthusiasm and commitment. Second, we must create an atmosphere that encourages our people to think in unusual and creative ways to be effective. Our government is responsible for setting the atmosphere for effective innovation. One key component of innovation is knowledge. The importance of knowledge cannot be stated enough. Our leaders must set forth one or more challenges to the citizens.

Without a challenge, there will be no drive to provide the impetus for creativity. It is crucial to the overall development of an individual and the society as a whole. Knowledge is the key to national recovery. In summation, education is one most important investments that the government can make for its people's future. Do we know that our societal segments are based more on our education than our economic worth? Daniel 9:2 says, "I Daniel understood by books." You see, Daniel was a reader, a researcher. When people say we are not a reading culture, that reveals a sign of ignorance, and ignorant people are always destroyed. God himself said it this way: "My people are destroyed for lack of knowledge" (Hosea 4:6). Most importantly, our government needs to find ways to shift our focus away from idleness and work out how to capture durability and flexibility of learning. Matthew 20:3, 6–7 says, "And he went out about the third hour and saw others standing idle in the market place; And about the eleventh hour he went out and found others standing around; and he said to them, 'Why have you been standing here idle all day long?' They said to him, 'Because no one hired us.' He said to them, 'You go into the vineyard too.'" We can liken the vineyard to Liberia, where most people have no skills or occupations and where most are unemployed. Therefore, they are involved with nothing but idleness,

The result is found in Proverbs 19:15, which says, "Laziness casts into a deep sleep, and an idle man will suffer hunger." The Scripture here is giving us a profound reflection on the hallway of life, decorated with gripping images of idleness on the edge of frustration and death —a reflection of the culture and country that is called Liberia, where the government's misguided leaders betrayed the gravity of our condition. Jesus is saying to us in Matthew 20:6–7 that despite the turbulence of purposeless living that causes so many of us to stumble aimlessly through life, we should not allow the conditions in our lives to distract us from the true meaning of our lives.

God has not given up on us, but through these hopeless situations, he wants us to see the pre destined purpose we were created for. The right environment will produce champions. A great number of our people are searching for a way to tune into what God has embedded inside of them. Life cannot be fictionalized because God created every life with a purpose, and it is that purpose we must give expression. There is no fulfillment in idleness. As the popular saying goes, idle hands are the devil's workshop. Idleness is a distraction and misconception of who you are. I think the government should set up schools and institutions to help us focus on developing the approaches that will best help students make progress. But tragically, those in leadership are ignoring this issue years after years. The government would benefit from the students by helping them learn more about their values and become increasingly skillful at expressing their growing understanding of the roles they play in the society. One of the ways we can create the right environment is by supporting the youth in improving their academic pursuits to make them better citizens. The errors that the government makes are compounded by the fact that representatives tend not to recognize the Word of God.

"The sluggard does not plow after the autumn, so he begs during the harvest and has nothing" (Proverbs 20:4). Let me give us some simple definitions. The word plow means "to proceed laboriously, to reinvest (earnings or profits) in one's business." Therefore, so many of our people are beggars. The right environment was never created to bring true equality to all our nation's citizens. This sort of condition has deafened many people to constructive input. In this process of national recovery, we need to first create the right environment to improve the quality of life. Our government needs to examine and improve the founding principles, not because these maxims are not good enough but because they can be even better.

Whenever government representatives step into power, they must fulfill their roles and influence the lives of the people they lead positively. Life offers more when the right environment is created. That's why America is the most powerful nation on this earth. They created the right environment for their people and even strangers who live on their shores. Whether the government is just starting out or starting over, I think it is time for our government to reset its priorities and clear the distractions and disruptions so that it can be a government of the people, by the people, and for the people, one that is answerable to the people. The term democracy comes from the Greek language and means "rule by the (simple) people." Guy Spire states that we think we control our environment, but in fact, it is our environment that controls us. Take any person, for example. Put the individual in the wrong environment, and he or she can get up to some pretty bad things.

No wonder we are the way we are. The government can still close the gap by caring and improving the well-being of its people. The right environment can positively represent both the government and its people. When people are in the wrong environment, they feel paranoid. It becomes a real struggle for anyone who has loads of ideas, talents, gifts, and dreams in a wrong environment. Your environment can facilitate or discourage interactions among the citizens. Your environment can influence the citizens' behavior and make them motivated to excel. People's suggestibility in the right environment can be powerfully influenced and can make them behave more competitively. Many people want to do something better with their lives, but they are unable because the wrong environment is a recipe for disaster.

Studies have revealed the dark future that our country will face if we do not change our dominant view of the government. In a country like ours, trees and green spaces provide much-needed peace and tranquility from the stress we go through on a regular basis. Our forests are vital to our existence. The result of imbalance is increasing the likelihood of extreme weather events in our nation. Deforestation has long posed a threat to our country.

Research shows that forests cover 30 percent of the planet's land and provide vital protection from sandstorms and flooding as well as the substantive natural habitat for wildlife. They are one of our greatest resources for offsetting some of our outrageous carbon emissions, and without the canopy of the forest, we leave areas vulnerable to intense heat. Deforestation can even indirectly cause everything from unexpected rainfall to extreme heat waves. This might not seem like a lot, but it can have devastating consequences for our country and the livelihoods of millions of our people, further driving climate change. Every single year we lose many areas because of deforestation, and these environmental issues affect us all. Power, greed, and politics are affecting this precarious environmental balance. But a few influential politicians are still attempting to undermine the climate change action and concern with misleading propaganda.

Research shows that this is a popular strategy for the logging industry and nations with a commanding interest in large forests. Many use corrupt means to gain access to our forests. Illegal logging contributes to deforestation. And it also causes the loss of biodiversity and undermines the rule of law. These illegal activities also undermine responsible forest management, encourage corruption, and tax evasion, and reduce the income of the producer countries, further limiting the resources producer countries can invest in for sustainable development. Now, this is our situation right here. Illegal logging has serious economic and social implications for the poor and disadvantaged. Millions of dollars' worth of timber revenue are lost each year. We've all heard it before, but really, we need to stop destroying them and start replanting. The refreshing and reassuring news is that we will control our future by controlling our environment. Creating the right environment by the government will ensure the protection of our children's future.

Genesis 1:28 states, "Be fruitful and multiply and fill the earth and subdue it, and have dominion over the fish of the sea and over the bird of the heavens and over every living thing that moves on the earth." Of course, some so-called Christians have misused the Bible to justify much cruelty. This passage does not teach that humans should be cruel to animals or the planet but that we should be stewards of it. In fact, at the end of human history, God will judge people based on how they treated the Earth. John writes, "And the nations were enraged, and Your wrath came, and the time came for the dead to be judged, and time came to reward Your bond-servants the prophets and the saints and those who fear Your name, the small and the great, and to destroy those who destroy the earth" (Revelation 11:18). The rampant environmental degradation taken place in Liberia today is one of the moral issues most ignored by Christians. It is evident in both the Old and New Testament that nature occupies a special place in the heart of God. As the psalmist indicated in Psalm 147, "All nature declares praise to God." If God cares so much about nature, we must too. But the destruction of nature shows disrespect for God and the environment he created. So, it also shows a lack of concern for the consequences that environmental destruction has on current and future generations.

Even after recognizing the biblical imperative for responsible care of the environment, it should not be difficult to translate this knowledge into action. God placed Adam in the garden of Eden just as he has placed us in Liberia. "And told him to dress it and to keep it" (Genesis 2:15). Jeremiah 2:7 says, "I brought you into a fertile land (Liberia) to eat its fruit and rich produce, but you came and defiled my land, and you made my inheritance detestable." Luke 16:2, 10, 13 shows us the consequence of not being a good steward. "And He called him and said to him, 'What is this I hear about you? Give an account of your stewardship, for you can no longer be a steward. He who is faithful in a very little thing is faithful also in much, and he who is unrighteous in a very little thing is unrighteous in much, you cannot serve both God and mammon.'" It's time to stop letting some of our politicians drag their feet and start pushing them to step up and lead. I have nothing but gratitude and respect for this country. I want to encourage national and corporate leaders to step up and take positive actions that will make a difference in the lives of the people. In Acts 20:22, the disciple Paul said, "I consider my life worth nothing to me, if I only may finish the race and complete the task."

Every one of us in this nation needs a purpose. Being in government without purpose (even with so much knowledge) can become mindless, heartless drudgery. But if you add purpose, you can make a significant impact and change this catastrophic disaster. Purpose gives you focus. Today Liberia is split into many compartments, and it looks like everyone has his or her own reigning force because of our lack of national purpose. Solomon had a national purpose to build a temple, not for his own glory but for the glory of a higher power and purpose. A prophet that was sent to the nation Israel had a goal, and in his mission, he would keep the entire nation from straying from its original purpose. The greatest thing the government can do is to give the people purpose. Without a continuous sense of mission and vision, life can become so demoralizing.

After Joshua led the Israelites into the Promised Land and accomplished his purpose, he resoundingly reminded the nation of the continuity of its purpose and need to carry that purpose to its next stage of development. If our government had a national purpose, the people would focus their attention. Let's do a case study on King David. The king, faced with the daunting task of the construction of a temple, handed it over to his own son, Solomon, who admittedly lacked experience in the construction business. But David had also given himself wholeheartedly to do this project. "With all my resources have I provided for the temple gold for gold work, silver for the silver, bronze, iron, onyx, stones of various colors, Besides I now give my personal treasures of goal and silver over and above everything I have provided for this holy temple Now who is going to consecrate himself today to the Lord?" (1 Chronicles 29:2–5).

What he meant was, "Who is going to follow my example and give their wealth and labor to help build this temple?" And because he put his money where his purpose was, he got a tremendous response

Then the leaders of the families, the officers of the tribes. … the commanders of the thousands and commanders of hundreds … gave willingly; They gave toward the work on the temple five thousand talents of gold, ten thousand talents of silver … eighteen thousand talents of bronze. Then the people rejoiced because they had offered so willingly for they made their offering to the LORD with a whole heart, and King

David also rejoiced greatly. The people willingly responded to their leader David. (1 Chronicles 29:6–9)

No leader ever unified the efforts of thousands of people or raised copious amounts of capital without an unwavering sense of purpose. King David had a national project to change his environment by building a temple. He solved the problem creatively by building synergies. This is the style of leadership that will bring a change of environment.

Let us consider the philosophy of Kōnosuke Matsushita, founder of the giant Japanese conglomerate that bears his name. "The mission of a manufacturer should be to overcome poverty, to relieve society from misery, and bring in wealth." Furthermore, it should contribute to the "progress and development of society and the well-being of people … thereby enhancing the quality of life throughout the world." When you change the environment, the environment will change the people. It is like a system. When you change the system, the system will change the people.

By drawing from the insights in this book, we can build a bright future for our children and the generation to come. II Chronicles 20:20 says, "They rose early in the morning and went out to the wilderness of Tekoa, and they went out, Jehoshaphat stood and said, listen to me, O Judah and inhabitants of Jerusalem, (Liberia) put your trust in the LORD your God and you will be established, put your trust in his prophets and succeed."

CHAPTER 17

The Liberian Dream

Please permit me to share with you I thought the Liberian dream should have been. A dream that we want to shine with resplendent light, a dream where our service could match our integrity, a dream of affordable housing. The Liberian dream was supposed to be a reality to assure economic prosperity and growth. But it has become an illusion and fantasy. The dream was all to serve a greater good to benefit its people. It was to be a dream of perpetual hope, prosperity, and excellence. It was a dream that was to provide a future and a hope for an entire nation, a dream where every Liberian who desired a better life and the pursuit of happiness had their chance. It was a dream to bring freedom and hope to all people as the lone star on the west coast of Africa. It was a dream to pursue happiness and the dignity of life. With this dream, we adopted a constitution that was very similar to that of the great United States of America. This Constitution guarantees that all are free and created equal. The Liberian dream fell off its track because most of the leaders did not have the nation at heart. They sought wealth and position instead.

The dream did not elevate the citizens. No, the leaders marginalized the citizens. If you elevate someone to a higher status, you consider him or her better or important. The dream slipped off its path and failed because of exclusionary governance and economic policies that still hurt Liberians. To have a dream for a nation, you must believe in the doctrine or ideology of nationalism. Nationalism comes from the word nation. A nation is a large aggregate of people united by common descent, history, culture, or language, inhabiting a particular country or territory. A nationalistic government would serve to establish laws and policies for the benefit of the citizenry. Nationalism is the belief that every nation has the right to rule independently the land that they have lived on. Our founding fathers declared independence in 1847 to ensure that our country stood as a free and independent state in Africa. Since the declaration, Liberia has contributed immensely to the independence of many nations in Africa and other parts of the world; however, our own country continues to experience backwardness, and its people live in abject poverty because of bad governance.

The dream was to turn the ordinary people into extraordinary people. But Liberians are devoid of their dreams because of unpatriotic and un-nationalistic leaders who only crave power. These dream killers have caused a general breakdown of the country's national determination in a changing world. A leader with a national dream can enable others to contribute to art, science, engineering, medicine, and geology. Because of the lack of nationalism, our country is being sold from under our feet by politicians who come to power. They just want to pursue their economic interests. A leader with a dream for the nation will oppose wars fought for reasons that do not affect our national interests. Many politicians ascend to public office just to implement what they have learned over the years—corruption and the repressive tendencies of successive regimes. Because of this trend, the dreams of many Liberians have become an illusion. In this process of national recovery, we want to look at the concept of a dream in the context of our nation.

Dreams reflect the direction you feel the country should take. It gives you the power to make the transition and envision yourself accomplishing that dream. As a leader, you must envision the success of those you lead in your dream. It becomes a reflection of the various aspects of life that we must develop. This will require death to the self. John 12:24 says, "Truly, truly, I say to you, unless a grain of wheat falls into the earth and dies, it remains alone; but if it dies, it bears much fruit." It is like the end of something old to make room for something new." When a leader comes to power, despite the commonality shared by many, it is important for the leader to interpret and share his or her dream and transmit a sense of urgency and enthusiasm to others. Many American presidents made an impact on their country as great communicators. John F. Kennedy,

Franklin D. Roosevelt, and Abraham Lincoln come to mind as examples. But only one president in the history of America was called the great communicator, and that was Ronald Reagan,

"Then Joseph told his brothers, 'Listen, I had another dream, and this time the sun and moon and eleven stars were bowing down to me.' When he told his father as well as his brothers, his father rebuked him and said, 'What is this dream you had? Will your mother and I and your brothers come and bow down to the ground before you?'" (Genesis 37:9–11). When a man had a clear dream from God, he was expected to share it with others, no matter how it impacted his own life. "Joseph told Pharaoh later when he had two dreams with the same message that the matter had been firmly decided by God, and God would do it soon" (Genesis 41:32). If Joseph believed that his own two dreams were sure to happen, he probably felt obligated to tell others. Joseph could communicate with maximum effectiveness. A leader with a dream possesses a clear vision, makes decisions easily, and delegates very effectively because of his or her uncanny ability to communicate when it comes to leading the country. The leaders know who they are, what they stand for, and what they want to be done because they have a dream and people will want to get on board with them, not because of their ability to impress people with big words or complex sentences but because of the effective communication of their dream. People will connect with them through the blueprint of their dream.

Effective leaders with a dream focus on the people who they're leading. They know it is impossible to effectively lead people without knowing something about them (i.e., their welfare and intellectual aspirations). They are concerned about the needs of the people and what needs to be accomplished for the people. People will believe the leader because the leader believed in the people. Leaders with a big dream communicate their dream by giving people something to feel, something to remember, and something to do. These leaders can express their dreams in such a way that people can understand, internalize, and implement them. I firmly believe if we dream to create an educated society that is highlighted and pursued, it will make a significant difference.

Liberia College, now the University of Liberia, established in 1862, is the second-oldest institution of higher learning in West Africa. The institution was founded by the Trustees of Donations for Education in Liberia. Simon Greenleaf, the Harvard College law professor who drafted Liberia's independence Constitution of 1847, was the founder and president of the trustees. I believe this represented a dream intended to shape us academically and prepare us for greatness. We should have invested in affordable and accessible quality early childhood education. We should have lowered tuition for higher education and make it available to everyone. We also had a dream for improving transportation, enhancing public safety, bringing county services to residents, supporting environmental stewardship, updating facilities, and connecting residents and business to government.

We had a dream of transparency where legislation required bills to be publicly posted twenty-four hours before a vote was taken. The government's failure to address long-standing inequalities has made it impossible for the Liberian dream to become a reality. This book is candidly describing the twists and compelling forces that have converged to make the Liberian dream hard to achieve. The new leadership in the new Liberia should develop a clear yet nuanced sense of what lies at the root of modern Liberia. When these concerns are addressed convincingly, it will give us a window into the realities of life in Liberia. I also dream that mandatory career planning will be instituted by the new leadership for all citizens so that all feel they have a chance to develop themselves and advance in life. There is another type of justice emphasized in the Bible—concern for the poor, the sick, and the disabled. In Ezekiel 16, the city of Jerusalem is compared with her sister, Sodom, whose inhabitants were "arrogant, overfed and unconcerned." They did not help the poor and the needy.

The question of "who gets what" has been debated since biblical times. The Bible has several passages that address the issue of what constitutes a fair share of the proceeds, harvest, or spoils of war. James 2:1–4 points out that rich and poor alike have rights. "If you show special attention to the man wearing clothes and say, 'Here's a good seat for you,' but say to the poor man, 'You stand there' … have you not discriminated among yourselves and become judges with evil thoughts?'" Our success is best if it is shared. This is the philosophy that helped Joseph devise his "fair share" plan so that his adopted country, Egypt, would not starve in the famine that was affecting the land. Again and again, Joseph could have victimized the Egyptians like our past leaders did, but again, he saved them from their lack of foresight. He wisely set aside a portion of the grain harvest before the famine and sold it to his countrymen when they ran out of grain, presumably at a fair rate of exchange. When they ran out of money, he exchanged the grain for their livestock, and when they ran out of livestock, he bought their land but gave it back to them for their use on the condition that they keep four-fifths of the harvest for themselves and give one-fifth to Pharaoh. I believe this is a dream for Liberia.

Joseph could have bled his adopted countrymen dry, but his overall scheme was just and fair to ensure that they would have enough productive and consumable resources to survive the famine and prosper again once it was over. Though he was a politician, he remembered to give the boss his fair share as well. Your dream for the nation as a leader becomes the Liberian dream. A leader with a great dream will treat all people with respect because of their basic human rights. The rules and procedures will be applied evenhandedly without favoritism across all segments of the nation. "David reigned over all Israel, doing what was just and right for all his people" (2 Samuel 8:15). Justice and fairness is a dream that many people in this country have never seen. But God shows us in his Word that it was and is still part of his plan for mankind, and if we will fulfill that dream, it has to be lived as prescribed. Psalm 106:3 says, "Blessed are they who maintain justice, who constantly do what is right." This is not the situation with us. The biblical pillars of integrity that were established as part of the Liberian dream have been compromised and corrupted. It seems like there are different sets of rules for various levels of people.

God is addressing the leaders of Israel here like he is addressing our leaders today. Micah 3:9–11 says,

Now hear this, heads of the house of Jacob and rulers of the house of Israel, who abhor justice And twist everything that is straight, Who build Zion [Liberia] with bloodshed And Jerusalem [Monrovia] with violent injustice, Her leaders pronounce judgment for bribe, Her priests instruct for a price And her prophets divine for money, Yet they lean on the LORD saying Is not the LORD in our midst? Calamity will not come upon us.

Micah 6:8, 12 says, "He has told you, 'O man, what is good; And what does the LORD require of you But to do justice, to love kindness,

And to walk humbly with your God? for the rich men of the city are full of violence, her residents speak lies, And their tongue is deceitful in their mouth.'" We can still achieve the Liberian dream in the foreseeable future. The new leadership must set up a system to counteract abuses of justice, even by those at elevated levels. In doing so, they are following the lead of Jehoshaphat, king of Judah, who set up a system of courts and advised the newly appointed judges, "Consider carefully what you do … Judge carefully, for with the Lord our God there is no injustice or impartiality" (2 Chronicles 19:4–11).

To accomplish the Liberian dream, the new leadership must be willing to make long-term economic sacrifices in the interest of fairness for the people. Therefore, people get angry and resent the government. Leaders with a dream for this nation will seek justice for all who are affected in this fractured country. A great leader with a dream will live the message of his or her dream. This leader will always ask a few trustworthy friends, a spouse, or a mentor whether he or she is living the dream, and these trustworthy people are able to see things that the individual is blind to. A great leader with a dream will receive the comments without defensiveness, and he or she will make changes for progress.

David was the great king of Israel with a dream, and Joab was a servant to David, who advised him. II Samuel 19:5–8 says,

Then Joab came into the house to the king and said, "Today you have covered with shame the faces of all your servants, who today have saved your life and the lives of sons and daughters, the lives of your wives, and the lives of your concubines, By loving those who hate you, and by hating those who love you, For you have shown today that princes and servants are nothing to you; for I know this day that if Absalom were alive and all of us were dead today, then you would be pleased, Now therefore arise, go out and speak kindly to your servants, for I swear by the LORD, if you do not go out, surely not a man will pass the night with you, and this will be worse for you than all the evil that has come upon you from your youth until now." So, the king arose and sat in the gate. When they told all the people, saying, "Behold, the king is sitting in the gate," then all the people came before the king. Now Israel had fled, each to his tent.

It is a good thing for a leader to initially pursue just policies and actions from the outset, but often a leader must have the courage to confront and reverse injustices, some of which may have been perpetrated by his own government. We are being poisoned with the luxury and corruption among the upper class, which is defined as dishonest or fraudulent conduct by those in power. It is a fatal disease called apathy, and it is sabotaging our well-being. I know this book will challenge the status quo. These are the hard truth that many people do not want to talk about. But it is a profound honor to have been chosen to share my thoughts with you. This is just yet another way to bring hope to a new generation and incubate the kind of innovation, creativity, and progress that Liberians yearned for. God is preparing this nation for greatness, even though we are being exploited by what I call "foreign interlopers" that are treating us unfairly by using our resources, works, and ideas and giving us very little in return for their personal gain. Empty politicians are upsetting the natural order of things.

I was watching a movie the other day, and I remember a guy talked about trust. Another person said, "Who needs trust when you have power?" This is the situation in Liberia. People cannot be trusted. I do not just believe in Liberia. I believe in the people who make Liberia. The name Liberia is supposed to represent our hopes and dreams. Though many people see Liberia as a hopeless war zone, I see a pasture, a breeding ground for artistry and greatness, and I know we can realize that dream in the future if we work now. Liberia will produce great leaders, presidents, UN secretary, generals, leaders in business, leaders in government, and more importantly, great people who will achieve their dreams, men and women who will bring about national development and change the course of history. I salute you. This book is an excellent start. The past is gone. The only direction for a dreamer is forward, never backward. It is your time, but time is precious. It should not be wasted. You can make it. It is a new day and a new season for Liberia. Welcome to your future. Go forth and embrace the future that awaits you, the Liberian dream.

CHAPTER 18

Prayer for Liberia

Liberia needs godly leaders with biblical values who understand the times we are living in and are willing to take a firm stand and act. Listen, Liberians. This is not a time to sit on the fence and wait to see what will happen; it is a time to fervently pray for change. An individual who prays and humbles him or herself before God can change the course of a nation like ours. Your prayers are so important, and together we can make an eternal difference in the nation. It is time to wake up and recognize the power God has placed in our hands and give our all to the purpose of God. Pray that God will release the spirit of repentance (2 Chronicles 7:14).

Pray that God will raise up righteous leaders who model integrity and authenticity (Ephesians 4:1–2; Proverbs 14:34). Pray that Liberians will see their spiritual poverty, that all citizens will awaken to their great spiritual need (Joel 3;12). Pray that godly men and women will be placed in positions of authority so that God's people can rejoice (Proverbs 29:2). Pray that leaders we elect will be just and fear God rather than men and depart from evil (2 Samuel 23:3; Proverbs 17:14). Pray that citizens will seek wise leaders who listen to biblical counsel (Proverbs 1:3–5). Pray that Liberians will vote with wisdom and discretion (Proverbs 3:21b). Pray that people will be able to see the truth (Psalm 86:11), that error will be exposed, and that people with wicked agendas will be made weak (Proverbs 25:5). Pray that Christians will speak the truth about those running for office (Ephesians 4:15). Pray for truth in the media (Proverbs 12:22). Pray that Christians will put their confidence in God rather than any political candidate (Psalm 118:9). Pray that Liberians will look to God to overcome the enemies of truth and righteousness (Psalm 60:11–12). Pray that God will work through leaders to keep the doors open for his gospel to be proclaimed (Colossians 4:3a).

I pray that all Liberians across the nation and other parts of the world will get on their knees and repent, not only of our own sins but of the sins of the whole nation, and I pray that God will answer our prayers. We do not need any political messiah (Colossians 2:8). I have found something that can bring the truth and bring change. And that is the Word of God. John 8:32 says, "You will know the truth, and the truth will make you free." Liberia will know the truth, and the truth will make our nation free.

Printed in the United States
By Bookmasters